LEARN TO BE A
GENERAL CONTRACTOR

Build Your Dream House
or Do a Renovation

Carl Heldmann

NPS
®

National Plan Service Inc.
Elmhurst, Illinois 60126

Acknowledgments

This book is authored by Carl Heldmann and his associates who are authorities on the subject.

Special National Plan Service Inc. Edition, May 1990

Published by Storey Communications, Inc., Schoolhouse Road, Pownal, Vermont 05261

Printed in the United States by Capital City Press

Designed and produced by Nancy Lamb

Edited by Constance L. Oxley

Contents

Preface

Carl Heldmann is a well-regarded licensed contractor, having demonstrated his skill in the construction field for a number of years in various geographic areas.

It is our opinion that houses will continue to rise in price. The continuing increase in cost will not be due to any one single factor. The increases relate to a number of occurrences such as the rising costs of labor, materials, land values, and interest. Many people are being squeezed out of the housing market today because of escalating building costs.

People, particularly young people, are eager to have homes of their own. A great many other people live in houses they don't like or houses that are too small for their needs. The individual wants to act now but is stymied by discouraging cost figures.

We offer a solution for you if you are willing to do a certain amount of legwork, by organizing, and using your common sense. The "how to" contained herein is not merely impressive but extraordinary. Two elements are required of you — planning and follow-up. What better way to employ your supervisory skills?

By using this book you will be taking yourself on a journey — a journey which will result in satisfaction of accomplishment as well as saving. We offer you a unique opportunity to build your own home or vacation home or addition, employing steps that hundreds of general contractors use.

It is not difficult and it is vastly rewarding! You won't be competing with any general contractor because you probably couldn't afford to build unless you acted as the general contractor. We will show you step-by-step how you can have a house by building it yourself, thereby saving thousands of dollars.

Capitalize on the opportunity to give yourself a better constructed home at a much lower cost. You have the need. We offer the solution in these pages. It's up to you.

We will also outline another way — using a general contractor as a manager, with you as the primary general contractor, still saving you thousands of dollars. What could be better than saving on construction costs and having fun doing it.

Whenever we use the term "build yourself," we do not mean the physical use of tools and materials. We mean that you will "build yourself" with you as the organizer of subcontractors who will do the actual physical labor. Most people don't realize that you don't have to have a general contractor's or builder's license to legally build a house. Anyone can obtain a permit to build a house on his or her own land. Whether you build your own permanent residence or that seemingly more elusive second home, or add a room, this book will save you money. We promise. You can do what others have already done.

Scores of people have successfully acted as their own general contractor and truly enjoyed it. They have been homemakers, jewelers, salespeople, engineers, bankers, truck drivers, lawyers, doctors, farmers, and many more from all walks of life. You can do it and enjoy the pleasure of accomplishment.

You don't really need a technical knowledge of building or be a super do-it-yourselfer. What you have to have is enthusiasm, a willingness to involve yourself in a project to get what you really want, and this book to guide you.

Our book does not concern itself with "how-to" build things such as patios, decks, and other projects. Nor is it a book on "how-to" be a handyperson, or a "how-to" do a variety of things. This is a book on "how-to" build your house by being your own contractor and save money. What better help could we give you? Good luck being your own contractor or renovator. National Plan Service is pleased that you have chosen this route to success.

Introduction

If you had to understand all the laws of physics that enable you to balance and ride a bicycle before you were allowed to ride or able to ride, it is doubtful that you would be interested in trying or learning. The laws are there and they work, therefore you can ride.

Well, if you had to know, or if most other general contractors had to know, all about such things as stresses, load bearings, and electrical wiring, very few of us would ever build. You will employ people who know their specific trades and have the expertise. You do not have to be an expert.

In this book we are brief and nontechnical about certain subjects because we don't want to frighten you away from looking at the overall picture. Haven't you ever been concerned about some other seemingly complex thing? "By gosh, if he can do it, so can I." It is really true in the case of building your own home. In this book, we are going to tell you how to get that dream home.

You will notice that some technical terms are set in *italics* in this book. They are terms you should understand. If you don't, look them up in the Glossary, where they are defined.

You will read several sample contracts we have provided to acquaint you with the legal language. **We urge you not to use the contracts unless you have reviewed them with your attorney.** State laws differ on what is required in such contracts, and your attorney will be familiar with such differences. Good luck and happy building!

Part I

BE YOUR OWN HOUSE CONTRACTOR

—————————————— CHAPTER 1 ——————————————

Saving Money

THIS IS A book that will teach you how to be a general contractor for your own house. There's one big reason for doing it — to save money. How much you will save will vary considerably depending on local prices for labor and materials, land costs, the size of the house, and your ability to follow the steps outlined in this book.

The size of the house will be the largest determining factor, as most general contractors base their profit and overhead on a percentage of the total cost. A larger house will cost more, and therefore will include a larger builder's profit and overhead. Real estate commissions saved will also be greater as the size of the house increases.

If you do all that I suggest in this book, a goal of 25 percent savings is possible, particularly if you are thinking of how much you will have to earn and pay taxes on to get the money to build your house. For some the savings may be less than 25 percent. But for all, those savings will be huge when you consider you won't have to pay interest on that amount over the long lifetime of your mortgage. The total is impressive. If you save $1,000 — and borrow that much less on a thirty-year, 15 percent mortgage — you will have to repay to your lending institution a total of $4,554 less. A dollar saved is $4.55 that does not have to be repaid. Actual cost estimating will be explained in Chapter 4.

Land costs alone can vary tremendously, and thus will affect the actual percentage of savings. They are discussed in Chapter 2.

Example 1

Example 1

A 1500 square foot ranch house with no garage or basement.

Retail at $50 per square foot	$75,000
Land cost	8,000
	$67,000
Actual direct cost at $35	52,500
You save approximately	$14,500
	Profit, overhead, real estate commissions

1

Example 2

Example 4

Example 2

A 2000 square foot two-story house with no garage or basement.

Retail at $50 per square foot	$100,000
Land cost	10,000
	$ 90,000
Actual direct cost at $35	70,000
You save approximately	$ 20,000
	Profit, overhead, real estate commissions

Example 4

A 3600 square foot two-story house with garage and unfinished basement.

Retail at $62 per square foot	$223,200
Land cost	30,000
	$193,200
Actual direct cost at $35 (heated area)	
500 square feet at $17.57 (garage area)	
1800 square feet at $5.37 (basement)	144,451
You save approximately	$ 48,749
	Profit, overhead, real estate commissions

Example 3

Example 3

A 2400 square foot two-story house with garage and unfinished basement.

Retail at $60 per square foot	$144,000
Land cost	18,000
	$126,000
Actual direct cost at $35 (heated area)	
500 square feet at $17.57 (garage area)	
1200 square feet at $5.37 (basement)	99,229
You save approximately	$ 26,771
	Profit, overhead, real estate commissions

What You Need to Know

You need to know very little about building to be a general contractor. You don't need to have the technical knowledge about framing or bricklaying or wiring. Your subcontractors will know their business just as mine do. I'll help you make sure of that.

You may wish to pick up some information on various aspects of building, and that's fine. In most bookstores there are excellent "how-to" books for the do-it-yourselfer on almost all phases of construction. You may want them. But there's no way you can become a master of all trades. The role of the general contractor — which you will be — is as an organizer, a manager, not a tradesperson. Your role is to get the job done — by other people.

Hire an Attorney

If, in any of the planning stages of building outlined in this book, you feel inadequate, hire a good real estate attorney. You will need the help of an attorney in certain steps anyway, such as in the closing of the loan. If you hire one now, the fee will be money well spent if it enables you to build your own home, and that fee is an actual cost of construction. Many attorneys will forgo hourly rates, or at least reduce them, if they are going to be involved throughout your project. Be sure you like the attorney in your first meeting. The two of you will have a long relationship, for the six or more months the house is under construction, so this is important. See Chapter 6 for information on obtaining an attorney.

If you can balance a checkbook, read, and deal with people in a fair manner, you can build your own house. Don't look at building a house as one huge job. I don't do this after eight years in the business. View each phase or step as a separate job and in this way the overall task will seem less monumental.

The most difficult things you will have to do will be behind you when you actually start construction. Sounds unbelievable, doesn't it? But it's true. Your job of planning and organizing will be 90 percent complete when you break ground, or it should be. At that point it is up to your team of experts — your subcontractors (subs) — to do its job. At least 99 percent of them will do their jobs correctly, even without you being at the site.

As you go along never be afraid to ask anyone a question about anything. Pride is foolish when it prevents you from asking a learning question.

Carpentry Crew

A definite help to you in building your own home, or even in helping you to make the decision to do so, is finding a good carpentry crew. The carpenter, or crew, is the key subcontractor. Having a good one before you start will help you make many intelligent decisions and will help your local lender to make a decision to lend you money. More on this later in this chapter.

A personal visit to a couple of building supply houses (usually the smaller ones) to ask for recommendations will give you more than enough leads to find a good carpentry crew.

If the first carpentry crew you find is too busy, ask them to recommend another. But usually another house can be worked into the first crew's scheduling. Your carpenter will be one of your best sources for finding many of your other subcontractors.

After selecting good candidates for this job, check them out. They should give you a list of four or five jobs they have handled. Talk to the owners. Look at the work they did for them. Others to check with are banks and building suppliers.

Just a note now about this key subcontractor. Most good carpenters have a very good knowledge of most phases of construction. They may be weak in their technical knowledge of electricity or mechanics, and may not be good at finances or management, but most have built a house or houses completely. The good carpenters are easy to find, hard to get, and usually worth waiting for. They will also cost you a bit more, but in the long run, will save you money and time.

KEEPING THE RECORDS

Unless you're an exceptionally orderly person, you'll find yourself with construction papers at your desk at home, more in your car glove compartment, and others scattered in pockets or your place of business.

Avoid this by organizing yourself early. Get a briefcase, which will be your traveling office file. Buy some manila folders, a dozen at least. Then label them as you need them. You'll need one for finances, another for inspections, with a schedule for those inspections made out by you, one for each of the subs — and more.

There are two reasons for doing this. First, it will keep your work flowing more smoothly if you don't have to paw through papers to find what you want. Second, there's a feeling of confidence that you will get just from seeing your part of the job arranged in such a businesslike way.

Time Involved

How much time is involved in being your own contractor? For each individual it will be different, but you'll spend more hours planning and getting ready than you will on the construction site; that is, if you let the subs do their jobs without your feeling that you must be there every minute.

In the planning stages you may spend a month of your spare time, or months, depending on how fast you are able to decide on all the various aspects that I will cover. For example, deciding on house plans can take an hour, a month, or even longer; the same thing is true with choosing land, specifications, and subcontractors.

The time involved after you start construction will be short. The maximum time ought not to exceed two hours a day; those hours need not interfere with your job or normal activities. You will have many helpers and free management. You can have real estate people (the ones you are dealing with on your lot) do some legwork by checking on restrictions, and getting information on septic systems and wells. Your suppliers can help you save time, too, by finding your subs for you, doing "take-offs" for estimating and ordering suppliers, and giving technical advice.

Get What You Want

This reminds me of a thought I will pass on to you. You will get more of what you want in your house, with fewer hassles, when you act as your own general contractor. Most contractors are very staid. They like to do things the same old way. This often causes problems for the buyer who wants something done a little differently. With you as the general contractor, you get things done as differently as you like.

One very simple and not too costly step you can take to save time and insure better communication is to put a phone on the building site. Long distance calls are easily controlled. In twelve years I've never had the job phone abused by a sub. It has saved me countless trips to the job site, too. Just be sure you or a sub takes the phone home each night.

Eight years ago I built a vacation home in the mountains about 140 miles from our permanent residence. I made only three trips to supervise and check on the progress the entire time the house was being built, from the staking of the lot to the final inside trim. I don't recommend this. I only mention it to show that you don't have to be there every minute or every day. My mountain house was built by phone. This was far cheaper and much less tiring than driving 140 miles each way. The subs did a beautiful job. They wouldn't have done any better if I had been there watching them.

Work by Phone

Phone calls to subs are the key to this business. Make those calls before they leave for work, or in the evening when you are not working. On-site inspections can be made by you before or after work or on your lunch hour. Daily on-site inspections usually aren't necessary. If you believe they are, and you can't do it, your spouse or a friend can. You don't have to be there every minute. There isn't a general contractor alive who is. For me that would mean that I could only build one house at a time and I'm usually building five or six.

You don't have to watch masons lay every brick or your carpenters pound every nail. You allow them to do their jobs. Mistakes may be made from time to time. Chances are they would have been made if you were there. There isn't a mistake in the whole process that can't be rectified. It should be your individual decision on how much time you want to be at the site.

You Can Get a Loan

Unless you are paying cash for your house, you will need a loan. Almost all loans for houses are made by savings and loan companies, banks, or mortgage companies.

For all practical purposes, getting your loan is the most important step, and the most crucial in building. No money, no house. You must determine very early in your decision-making process whether you will be able to get a loan.

The intricacies of financing are explained in Chapter 3, where we discuss how a loan works and how much you can borrow. I will be very honest and say that most lenders will be somewhat reluctant to lend to an individual who plans to be his or her own general contractor. This reluctance is legitimate. Lenders want to be sure the house will be built properly, and most important, finished. They don't want to step in and finish a house. They are lenders, not builders, and that's the way they would like to keep it. It will be a challenging sales job convincing them you can be your own general contractor, but with the knowledge you will receive from this book, you can do it.

Plan your visit carefully. You want to appear to be a person who has thought through all steps in the construction of the house, who understands the problems and has solutions to them. You know the banker won't be enthusiastic about your decision to be your own contractor, so you must do all in your power to present this approach as an asset, not a liability, and your projected savings can make it an asset.

The banker will wonder whether you are an organized person who can handle the details of home construction. You will be convincing if you have all of your homework completed when you reach the bank. "Make it look as though the only step left is to get the money," suggested one banker.

Information You Need

Your presentation should include a package of material. It must include the following:

1. Proof of your current income. Include joint incomes from all sources.

2. Good credit references.

3. A financial statement of what you own and what you owe.

4. Sufficient knowledge about being your own general contractor.

Numbers 1, 2, and 3 are prerequisites to buying or building under any circumstances. Number 4 is what this

MORTGAGE APPLICATION

Date: _____
Dept: _____
Branch: _____
By: _____
Ext: _____

No. _____

Mortgagee _____   Property Address _____

Co-Mortgagee _____

Street _____

AMOUNT & TERMS REQUESTED

Service Charge	Mtg. amt.	Int. rate	No. of months	Monthly Payt. prin & int.
	$	%		$

City _____

State _____ Zip Code _____

Phone No. _____ Bus. Phone _____

☐ Wood siding	___ Stories	___ Bedrooms	☐ Store Rm.	Utilities Public Comm. Individual		Type of Heating
☐ Wood shingle	☐ Split level	___ Liv. room	☐ Util. Rm.	Water ☐ ☐ ☐		_____
☐ Asb. shingle	___ % Basement	___ Din. room	☐ Garage	Gas ☐ ☐ ☐		Type of Paving
☐ Fiber board	☐ Slab on ground	___ Kitchen	☐ Carport	Elect. ☐ ☐ ☐		_____
☐ Brick or stone	☐ Crawl space	___ Fam. Rms.	___ No. cars			☐ Curb & Gutter
☐ Stucco or c. blk.		___ No. Rms.	☐ Built-in	Sanit.	Sept. Cess tank pool	☐ Sidewalk
☐ Comb. types	___ % Non-resid.	___ Baths	☐ Attached			☐ Storm Sewer
☐	___ Living Units	___ ½ Baths	☐ Detached	Sewer ☐ ☐ ☐ ☐		

LOT DIMENSIONS: Ft. x   Ft. =   Sq. Ft.

GENERAL LOCATION: _____

Year Built _____

ANN. R. EST. TAXES $ _____ **ANN. FIRE INS. $** _____ **SALE PRICE $** _____

Occupation of Applicant_____

Legal Description of Property_____

Occupant _____ Phone No. _____

Appraiser can gain access as follows: _____

What is your interest in this property? ☐ Titleholder   ☐ Purchasing on Land Contract   ☐ Purchase Agreement Attached

Seller _____ Phone No. _____

Broker _____ Phone No. _____

COSTS:	**NEW CONSTRUCTION**	**EXISTING CONSTRUCTION**
Lot Purchased ___ 19 ___ Price Paid $ ___		Date Purchased _____
Cost of Building	$ ___	Purchase Price $ _____
	TOTAL $ ___	

Continued on page 6

MORTGAGE APPLICATION continued

(FOR BANK USE ONLY)

Appraisal Requested By: _____ Date _____

Signature

_____

RECOMMEND	APPROVAL

☐ Pmts. 1/12 tax, fire ins. & FHA ins.
☐ Pmts. 1/12 tax
☐ Plans & Specs and Certificate of Occupancy
☐ Final inspection
☐ Advance when enclosed
☐ Completion of repairs _____

Loan   Service Charge
Percentage

_____

Mtg. amt.	Int. rate.	No. of months	Monthly Payt. prin. & int.
$	%		$

☐ Special conditions _____

_____

_____

BY: _____ Date _____

_____

book is all about. The lender will check out your knowledge of what I cover in each of the chapters. He or she will easily recognize your ability to estimate, find a lot, and select plans, and your knowledge of construction loans, permanent mortgages, subcontractors, suppliers, and the different phases of construction. Don't worry. All of these items are explained in this book.

Recently I discussed this matter with the lender with whom I do a great deal of my business. He is from a savings and loan firm that has a self-admitted reputation for being conservative. He said the firm would approve a loan if the individual showed sufficient evidence of being able to act as a general contractor. The ability to estimate fairly accurately and line up a few major subcontractors and suppliers were major considerations.

Don't Be Discouraged

All of the requirements for showing sufficient knowledge are covered in this book. There should be no reason for you not to get a loan. However, you should keep in mind that you may get turned down by one or two lenders before you get an approval. Don't be discouraged. Sometimes it is nothing more than personal chemistry, or other trivial things, and has nothing to do with your ability.

It costs nothing to go through the initial stages of discussion with a lender, and you may get a commitment for a loan. In building my first house thirteen years ago, before I was a general contractor, I was turned down by four lending institutions before I found two who would permit me to be my own general contractor. If I hadn't been persistent, who knows where I would be right now. I believe I was turned down because I didn't know everything you'll know when you finish reading this book. I didn't show sufficient knowledge until after the third rejection. Each time I was turned down, I would do a little more homework and had more confidence in myself. I didn't have a book — you do. You can do it.

Let's suppose you get turned down by everyone — a highly unlikely supposition, but perhaps you live in a small town and there are only two savings and loans and both are ultraconservative. Well, assuming your credit is good and you can afford what you have in mind, probably the only reason you can't get your loan is that the savings and loan officials just don't want you to be the general contractor. They're afraid — afraid you may not finish the job and this fear may be more real in a small town. Or they may be afraid of upsetting their favorite general contractors/clients. At any rate, if all or any of this is a problem, I recommend having a local attorney who specializes in real estate go to bat for you. It may cost you a few dollars — get an estimate — but don't forget, you'll be saving thousands. The local attorney's influence and expertise may sway the case. It's worth fighting for.

ANOTHER BANKER'S VIEWS

Bankers, I've learned, don't differ too much across the country. They tend to be wary when you mention being your own general contractor. They're willing to be cooperative if they think you have a good chance of finishing the job, but they don't want to be stuck with a half-completed house.

A New Englander banker quickly rattled off the three points we've already listed as requirements, covering credit references, a financial statement, and proof of income.

I asked what would make him more warmly disposed toward the would-be general contractor. He listed these points:

1. Own your lot, free and clear.
2. Proof of ability to handle the construction, as described in this book.
3. As much planning completed as possible, to assure the banker that this is not an idle dream, but a project that only lacks the needed financing. Such planning would include a set of house plans, tentative arrangements with suppliers, including estimates of the costs of the materials, and all information needed on such subjects as availability of utilities, any zoning restrictions, and regulations of the building inspectors.

An Alternate — The Manager's Contract

When you act as your own general contractor you must do a good selling job to the lender. And, after that, let's suppose the worst happens. You can't get a loan if you are the general contractor.

Or let's suppose you simply don't feel able to deal with subs.

Here are three other ways you can build, each using a general contractor in a position of increasing responsibility and cost to you:

1. A manager's contract.
2. Cost plus a percentage or a fixed fee contract.
3. Contract bid.

These are listed in the order that they usually increase costs to you. Since each one increases the contractor's responsibility, it will increase the cost of having that contractor. The only things that will now fluctuate are profit and overhead. The cost of the house, land, and other fixed expenses should remain the same.

For all practical purposes 2 and 3 are readily available contracts and are used by most builders with varying degrees of legalese and varying degrees of slant favoring one or the other parties. (Samples of all three are shown in the Appendix.)

The least expensive way to go and a way by which you can still be considered the general contractor and be accepted by your lender, and possibly feel more comfortable dealing with subs, is using the manager's contract, option 1.

My conservative lender said, "With a manager's contract, we definitely would make a loan."

Under this arrangement, you have a licensed general contractor who has one responsibility, to act as your manager with the subs. This contractor, in return for about one-third to two-thirds of his normal fee or profit and overhead, will assist in finding the subs (although you can still find your own), will schedule subs, check the quality of their work, approve the quality of materials, and order materials, when needed, in your name. You will be responsible for securing suppliers, permits, loans, paying all bills, including subs, and inspections for quality and approval. You will be responsible for the final job and its overall acceptance.

Some of the advantages of this contract are:

1. He/she will do a cost estimate.
2. He/she will help find subs.
3. He/she will schedule your time better.
4. He/she will help cut red tape and get the necessary permits.
5. He/she will arrange for temporary services.
6. He/she will schedule subs, from survey to landscaping.
7. He/she will develop materials lists.
8. He/she will assist in reviewing bills when requested.

A slight change from this procedure would be to hire a designer-builder who would advise you on plans, make any necessary modifications to those plans, review the specifications for such things as adequate insulation or the possible use of native materials, and inspect the process of construction.

In either case, the manager's contract in the Appendix could be modified to include more or fewer of the responsibilities of the general contractor. The cost, of course, will vary with the number of responsibilities listed.

If you decide to use one of the contracts in the Appendix, go over it with your attorney to check it for applicability and to make certain it conforms with local laws.

CHAPTER 2

Where to Start

YOU'VE MADE YOUR decision to build. Wonderful. You'll do well, so don't worry. What comes next? Well, where do you want to live, based on your needs and desires and finances?

Remember, in making this decision, that you can use this house as a stepping stone. Once you've built your own home, you can move up to a bigger or better house or location and possibly at no — and I mean no — extra cost. Each time you move you are adding to your profit as a builder, and thus are increasing your own *equity*.

Land

If you have lived in a city or town for a while, you should know where you want to build. If you haven't looked around, or if you are new to an area, I suggest using a local real estate broker. These brokers know what each area offers and what lots cost in different locations. If acreage is what you are after, here, too, a real estate broker is most helpful. Don't forget, your broker is one of those helpers I mentioned. A broker can help you locate the property you want, and can help with all the details necessary to assure you that it is a suitable building site. The broker should be able to show you a map of the lot, and point out the boundaries to you during a walk around the lot.

If you don't already own land, first choose the area where you want to live. Next, look for a site with acreage in that area, one that is suitable to build on.

Sloping Lots

If you want a basement and you live in an area of the country as I do where the soil doesn't drain well, you should avoid flat lots. A sloping lot will provide drainage by means of footing drains. If you want a basement, sloping lots are best in any part of the country. They assure drainage no matter what type soil, and they allow for one side or more of the basement to have good window areas for light and dryness. Also, in some areas the open side can be *frame construction*, which is a little less expensive than foundation brick or concrete block.

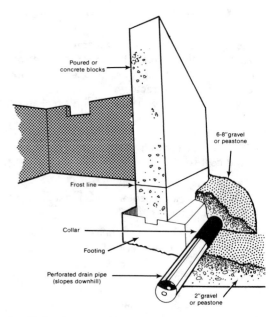

Footing drain will help to keep your cellar dry.

If you don't want a basement, try to find a relatively flat lot so that you won't have an excessive amount of *crawl space* (of fill, if you decide on a *slab foundation*). Crawl space is cheaper than a basement, and if the lot slopes, even excessively, only on one end or one corner, the cost of accommodating a foundation to that lot should not be increased too much. Notice I say "accommodating a foundation to that lot." So many people put the horse before the cart. I can't say strongly enough: find the land first and then the plans to fit.

In colder regions, south-sloping lots are becoming increasingly popular. They're ideal for solar homes, and offer protection from the chill of north winds.

DO YOU NEED A BASEMENT?

Do you want — or need — a basement?
Here are the arguments for and against a basement.

FOR

It's relatively inexpensive, compared with above-ground space, and particularly if you must dig down six or more feet anyway for placing footings and foundation walls, as you must in some parts of the country.

It gets your heating system and sometimes the fuel supply out of the way.

It's a good storage space, but may be too damp for paper, metal, and clothing.

It may provide you with garage space.

It's an excellent space for an out-of-the-way family room.

AGAINST

If the water table is high, flooding may be an annual headache.

It may be too damp for many uses, or require a dehumidifier.

It's an ideal spot for storing things better taken to the dump.

Building a basement can be expensive, particularly if the lot has an underground ledge, or the area is sometimes flooded.

Water and Sewage

Both water and sewage must be considered as you select your lot.

If both are provided by your city or town, you need only find out how you tap into them, and the costs involved.

If either one is provided (and quite often it is only water), your problem is slight. You may need some form of a permit, plus a percolation test for a septic system, to determine whether the soil will absorb the discharge of the system.

If you must provide both, some study is needed.

A septic system consists of a sewage pipe from your home to the septic tank, which is usually a large concrete box. Sewage enters this box and is broken down by bacterial action. A liquid then flows from the tank into a system of perforated pipes that permits the liquid to seep out underground in an area called a leach field. The size of the field required depends on the amount of sewage going into the tank, and the ability of the soil to absorb moisture. Sand is best; clay creates a problem.

Regulations in many regions require that a well be a certain distance, say a minimum of 150 feet, from your leach field, or the field of any neighbor.

Thus it's best to have a large lot if you must provide both water and a sewage system.

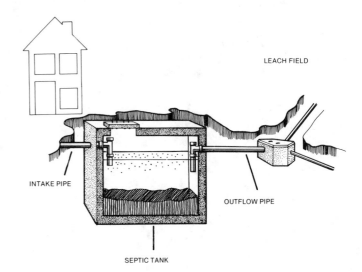

LEACH FIELD

INTAKE PIPE

OUTFLOW PIPE

SEPTIC TANK

Digging a well can be expensive. You can get a dowser, complete with forked branch, to "locate" water for you, or you can do what most well diggers do, and that is to locate the well where it's most convenient, and start digging.

Most well diggers charge by the foot of depth they bore and usually can estimate about how far they will have to dig. Some diggers will offer you a contract price for the well.

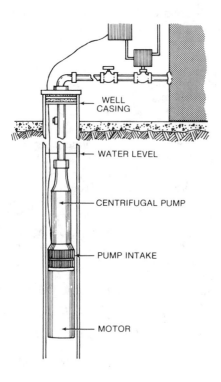

A common type of installation in a home well. The pump and motor are positioned at the bottom of the well.

Trees Are Valuable

If you like trees, try to find a wooded lot within your budget. Barren lots are cheaper to build on, but more costly to landscape — almost a direct cost wipe-out. A wooded lot generally costs 10 percent more to buy, $1,000 more to build on, and $1,000 less to landscape. It's your choice, but if you are concerned about top dollar resale in the near future, put a few thousand dollars extra into a wooded lot.

If the area in which you are looking has no development activity near it, I most strongly recommend *test borings* of the soil, before you purchase the lot, to determine its *load-bearing capabilities*. It will also show whether there is ledge on the site that might require blasting. This test is not expensive and one the seller should be willing to pay for. I have spent extra hundreds of dollars on *footings* due to poor soil. In some parts of the country, I'm sure that could have been thousands. Be sure that this test is included as a contingency in any contract to buy. It can also be included as a refund provision in the contract in the event that non-load-bearing soil is discovered after purchase.

If sewer and water facilities are not available on the lot, the contract should have a contingency as well as a refund provision regarding septic tank and well use. In some states this is a law. Land must be suitable to accommodate a septic system. The suitability is determined by local codes, but generally it is based on how quickly the soil drains. A soil test determines suitability.

Specialists in test boring for load-bearing are listed in the Yellow Pages under "Engineers, Consulting" or "Engineers, Foundation." Most county health departments make soil tests for septic systems. This is done for free, or at a very low cost. These departments also provide information about wells.

Let Broker Do Work

Put the burden of getting these tests on your real estate brokers. Let them do the legwork and checking. Just make sure it's in the contract you're offered. Let them earn their commissions. Let them hand you a nice, clean finished deal — a lot ready for you to build your dream house on.

If you deal with a Realtor — a member of the National Association of Realtors — you have a recourse if there is any problem, and that is the association. In almost all towns and cities the local Board of Realtors is so image-conscious and worried about a member ruining that image that it will protect you, the buyer. Simply call the board if you believe a Realtor isn't doing his or her job, or isn't representing your best interests.

Labels on figure:
WELL CASING
WATER LEVEL
CENTRIFUGAL PUMP
PUMP INTAKE
MOTOR

Zoning

Consider *zoning* when you are choosing a lot or acreage. Be aware of what could come into your future neighborhood — stores, offices, trailer parks, or industry. Look at what is already there. Such things as dumps, railroads, and industrial buildings make the lot worth less as a site for a home. One could write a book on zoning — and many have. A quick consultation with your real estate broker and your attorney should resolve any fears you have.

If water and sewer are provided, be sure your real estate broker (or you, or your attorney, if no broker is used) checks out all costs to get the water and sewer to your property line if it is not already there (it may be across the street), and any and all tap-in fees or privilege fees charged by the municipality or association providing the services. Do the same for gas, electrical, and phone services.

Checking out wells, septic system, load bearing, water and sewer fees, and zoning may take a few weeks. If you like the lot and don't want to risk losing it, you can make an offer with the understanding that your binder or deposit will be refunded if the conditions mentioned above are not in your favor. Don't put more than 10 percent down as a binder or deposit, and if using a broker, be sure the money is held in escrow. Above all, consult your attorney before closing a deal on any piece of land. I could say 100 times, and it wouldn't be enough. Have your attorney check the title to the lot, to make sure it is clear. Check out all restrictions on the size and type of dwelling you can build, and what a neighbor may build. This may or may not be covered in zoning. Different parts of the country use different means to protect an area from visual blight. Again, your broker and your attorney can help you on this.

How Much Should You Spend?

Land costs probably vary more than any item in the construction business. A small lot can be $6,000 or $60,000. An acre (43,560 square feet) of land can be $1,500 or $15,000 or more. Demand determines land prices. The more popular an area, the more demand for its lots and the higher the price.

How much you spend is really up to you. As you saw in the four examples in Chapter 1, the more expensive houses were built on more expensive land. This is generally the case, but not necessarily the rule. You can build house #4 out in the country, for example, on a less expensive acre of land. All of the examples in Chapter 1 were city lots with water and sewer. A well and septic tank for a country lot or acreage will cost several thousand dollars in most parts of the country, making that cheaper land a little more expensive.

Summing up, I would not let the cost of land exceed 25 percent of what the house alone will cost. Ideally, I try to stay in the 15–20 percent range.

You should have in writing all transactions about land. Most states require this in order for a transaction to be legal. Consult your attorney and you will be more than protected.

CHECKLIST FOR BUYING A LOT

Here are some of the many things you will want to check before buying a lot:

Neighborhood
Will your house fit in with others on street? _____
Quality of schools _____
Attractive street? _____
Transportation
Public transportation available? _____
Pollution (air, water, noise, such as airport) _____
Zoning restrictions _____
Sewage, water available _____
Soil tests made _____
Direction of slope, if any _____
Drainage (see after heavy rain, if possible) _____
Test borings _____
Size of lot _____
Trees (Valuable, but sun needed for garden) _____
Title Clear _____
Cost (Counter offer of 10–20 percent below asking price is often accepted.) _____

The House Plans

There are two accepted ways of obtaining house plans. Find a plan suitable for you and your house site by examining books containing plans. The other, and most expensive, is to have plans drawn for you by an architect.

Home Planbooks, featuring hundreds of designs, are available from National Plan Service, 435 West Fullerton Avenue, Elmhurst, Illinois 60126.

National Plan Service has provided plans for home building for over 70 years. The plans are used in all areas of the country so they are very carefully detailed to make them clear and concise. National Plan Service planbooks are found at lumber dealers and home center stores.

When you are ready to build, your lumber dealer can give you valuable cost-saving assistance about materials and local home building requirements. You should try to conform with the plans as drawn. Obtain advice from an architect on any changes, no matter how minor. An architect can advise you on the practicality of the changes you suggest and the additional cost, if any, of those changes. They are also familiar with local building code requirements.

Make Changes Early

Try to make all changes in the plans before you start construction. You need not have the plans redrawn for minor changes such as moving, adding, or deleting a window or door. But you should if you move walls, or change roof lines and roof pitches.

If the draftsman/designer redraws the plans, it will cost by the square foot for a finished product, including six to eight sets of the plans. If he or she designed your house from scratch, you could expect to pay about twice as much per square foot. In that case you usually would get more precisely what you wanted.

You could hire an architect to do this work. This would cost considerably more. Either one can do the job and either one should give you a quote over the phone of approximate costs. Look for names in the Yellow Pages or get recommendations from friends. Shop for price. Before you select an individual or firm, ask to see work done, and be sure to ask for a few references. Don't be timid and most of all, don't be intimidated. After all, you will be the employer. On-the-job changes are expensive, so make your decisions on paper and live with them or expect high cost overruns.

I usually rough sketch my houses on quarter-inch graph paper, and make most of my changes in this stage. If you plan to start from scratch with your plans, you can do this, too. A twelve-by-twelve foot room will be drawn three squares by three squares. This doesn't allow for wall thickness, and I don't in the early planning unless there's a tight squeeze with a roof or a stairway and I need to know then that it's going to fit. If this planning makes you feel uncomfortable, don't do it. Buy your plans or have them drawn for you from the sketching stage up. I only do it because I enjoy it. It really is a job for one of your subs, your architect, or draftsman/designer.

Stay closely involved with this phase, even if you don't sketch the plan. Pay strict attention to what is in the floor plans. Picture yourself walking through the house from room to room. If in doubt as to whether a room is large enough, find a room of about the same size, and compare.

This is a good time to mention the only two tools you'll need as a general contractor: two steel tape measures, one twenty-five feet long, and the other 100 feet. You may not use them many times, but they will help you eliminate guesswork in the planning stages.

CUTTING CONSTRUCTION COSTS

Your first chance to save a lot of money is now, when you are selecting the plans for your home.

• Do you need that many square feet? Every reduction you can make in size will cut the costs.

• One story or two? It's cheaper to build the same number of square feet of housing in a two-story house.

• What is its shape? A simple rectangle is the cheapest to build. Additional corners add to the costs.

• What style roof? The least expensive is the common gable roof.

• How's your timing? If you're building when there's a lull in construction, chances are you'll get your money's worth — and maybe a bit more.

Studying Plans

Figuring out the plan is easy, although it may look difficult at first. You'll be looking first at room sizes, room placement, traffic flow, kitchen work flow, closet space, number of baths, and overall size. Those are the major functions of design. Without too much effort you can move doors and windows, add them, or delete them on paper.

Unless you have an unlimited budget, and very few of us do, a house is a series of compromises. We can't afford all of those beautiful things we see in idea magazines. A house is going to cost so much per square foot using the average number of windows and doors and average appliances. If you **want** a Jacuzzi bath and can't afford it, compromise on something else — the size of the house, the garage, or a paved driveway.

Don't make any of your decisions a "matter of life and death." You may be surprised how unimportant that "big decision" was when you are finished. Agonizing over decisions only leads to friction — within yourself and with others. Make all of your decisions conscientiously but quickly, and them move on.

Be sure plans include specifications (specs). Specifications are lists of materials that are going into your house. Most plans come with a set of specs. Your draftsman or architect will include a set with the drawings.

There will be a "for input" in the specs for you. (Refer to the Appendix and you will see that these are places indicating decorative items, such as wallpaper, carpet, paint, stain, and door hardware.) Obviously, you will choose these. Since specs come early in the game, most people haven't selected these decorative items. Therefore, monetary allowances are used with the term "or equal." This means that the actual item finally selected, such as a kitchen faucet, will be of an approximately equal dollar amount and of similar quality to the one in the specs.

The amounts I have indicated in the specs will be found to be generally applicable. They are based on house size and price and they are easily upgraded or downgraded. They will vary per year depending on the inflation rate.

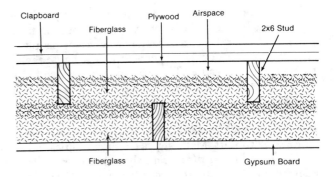

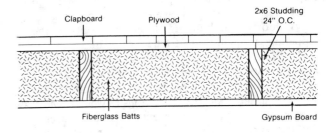

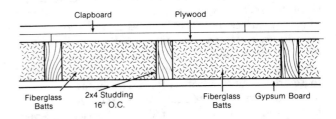

Three ways (and there are many more) of building outer walls, and their R-factors. At top, this has an R-factor of about 33, with the 2x6 studs not touching both the inner and outer layers. Center, with 2x6 studding, is about R-22. Lower is about R-13, and shows the older conventional method.

INSULATION

You're lucky. While those of us who own pre-1970s homes wish we had a chance to increase the insulation in them, you are starting fresh, and can plan a home that is energy efficient.

Consider this as you select your plan, and as you talk over your plans with your subs, particularly your carpenter and your insulation sub. There are decisions you can make that will result in thousands of dollars of savings as you live in your home over the years. Some decisions will require changes in your house plans and specifications.

If you have a full basement, should you insulate it? Do your windows provide two layers of glass? How will your outer walls be built? (Three possibilities are shown.) How much insulation will you have over your head? Will your heating ducts and hot water pipes be insulated? Is your chimney inside the house, where any heat it collects will be returned to the house, or on an outer wall, and thus causing a high heat loss? Does your fireplace provide a source of outside air, so that you're not wasting heated air, and does it have a tight damper, so hot air isn't flowing up it when the fireplace isn't in use?

You'll find utility companies discuss R-factor. This refers to the ability of a material to resist the escape of heat. A high R-factor means that you are not losing as much heat. There are standards of R-factors for walls and roofs that vary geographically.

Parts of Plans

Be sure your plans include the following pages, all of which are shown here or in the Appendix:

1. A *plot plan.* If your plans are drawn locally, the designer can prepare this plan for you. Otherwise you or a surveyor will have to do it. It is merely a plat or map of your lot with the position of the house drawn or blocked in. Its purpose is to insure that a given house plan will fit on a given lot. If it doesn't fit on paper it surely won't fit in reality.

First, the lot is drawn, then all the setbacks required by zoning and/or restrictions are sketched in, then the location of the house is indicated. The exact location may be slightly different when the house is physically staked out, but will be close to the indicated plat position — especially if it is a tight fit. If you have a lot consisting of several acres, the actual position of the house from that indicated on the plat could be changed by many feet.

The plat or plot plan won't be drawn first if you have a set of plans but no lot. It's better to find a lot first, then plans to fit. That is not an absolute rule. Some people love a set of plans or they want a particular house they have seen in a magazine. They would rather search for a lot to fit the plans. It can be done.

2. Spec sheets. In these lists of materials for your house, spell out as much detail as possible. Using an existing set (such as those found in the Appendix) is the easiest way to start. Make any necessary modifications.

3. Foundation plan. This shows the overall dimensions of the house and the locations of all load-bearing requirements, such as *piers*, steel, *reinforcing rods*, vents, basement slabs, and if a basement house, all walls, windows, doors, and plumbing of that basement. (In the Appendix you will find a foundation plan.)

4. Floor plans. You must have a plan for each floor. It will show outside dimensions, plus locations of windows and doors, plumbing fixtures, and large appliances. You may add the electrical drawings as well. These drawings show the locations of receptacles and switches. It is not necessary to have these shown. After a house is framed, you can go through it with an electrician and position receptacles and switches. However, for the purpose of getting quotes or bids from subs, it is best to have the electrical requirements included either in the floor plans or on a separate sheet. The same is true for heating and cooling (mechanical) requirements. It is best to have these drawn out in advance, for bid purposes and to locate the furnace. I use heat pumps exclusively in my houses so I don't have to worry about furnace placement. With wood, coal, gas, or oil planning the *flue* location is necessary, especially in a house without a basement and/or in a two-story house.

5. Detail sheet. This is a sheet showing cabinet details, cross sections of the inside of the house if there is a section that may not be perfectly clear from the floor plan, wall sections to show all the materials that make up a wall, such as brick, sheathing, studs, insulation, inside wallboard or paneling. A detailed section of a foundation wall is sketched to show proper construction technique, drainage, and waterproofing.

6. Outside elevations. These are the sheets (usually two) that show an outside view of how the house will look when finished. Usually all four sides are shown.

You'll need about six sets of plans, one for yourself, one for your lender, and one for each of the major subs. If you can get sets of plans that are inexpensive, it's good to have as many as possible. If you're going out for bids, for example, for work by a sub, each of the bidders should have a copy of the plans to study.

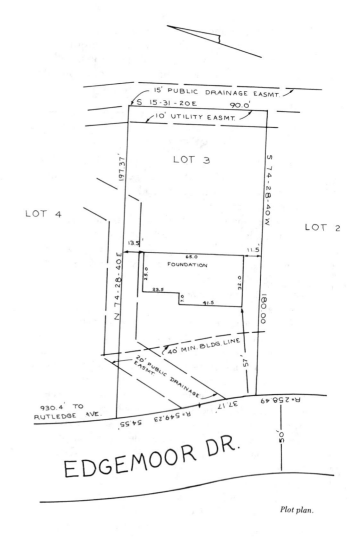

Plot plan.

CHAPTER 3

Financing

IF YOU FOLLOWED the instructions in Chapter 1, by now you have convinced a savings and loan, a bank, or a mortgage company to give you a loan. That loan will be divided into two phases:

1. The construction loan.
2. The permanent mortgage loan, to be paid off in twenty to thirty years.

Usually any difficulties in obtaining a loan involve the first phase, the construction loan, not the permanent loan given when the house is finished.

The Construction Loan

If you were able to secure a $60,000 mortgage for your new house and the lender were to give you a check for that amount before you started, both you and the lender would be in trouble. The lender, because he or she just loaned $60,000 on a house that doesn't yet exist; you, because you'd have to pay interest and principal on $60,000 before you even broke ground for that new house.

Considering varying interest rates, that could mean you would have to pay $800 a month on a nonexistent house, along with your regular monthly fixed expenses such as food and rent.

Enter the construction phase of mortgage loans — the construction loan. When you are approved for a mort-

gage for a house yet to be built, the lender will set up your loan first on a short-term basis, called the construction loan. The money is disbursed to you as the house progresses.

Only Interest Paid

You only pay interest, no principal, on the total amount lent to you for any given month during construction. For example, if the house is 20 percent complete after the first month, the lender, after a physical inspection of the progress of construction, will advance 20 percent of your total to you to pay your bills. If your total mortgage is, say, $60,000, then you will receive $12,000.

The house is now 20 percent complete, you are one month along in progress, and you have paid no interest yet. You won't have to until next month, when you will then pay the interest, say 16 percent for thirty days, on the $12,000 you received. That payment will be $160.

This is extremely important. Many people are afraid they will face two house payments at the same time. Not so. You use dollars that were advanced for construction to pay the monthly interest. You make no repayment of principal. You do not use your money. Construction loan interest is a cost of construction, part of the cost of any new home, whether you build it or I build it for you. It's not even part of the builder's overhead. It's a cost like lumber and nails. It is the second item on the estimate sheet in Chapter 4. Treat it as such and plan for it, along with other financing charges, and it won't bother you. Think of all the money you are saving by being your own general contractor.

DISBURSEMENT SCHEDULE

INSPECTION REPORT   DATE _____ Loan No. _____

Borrower _____

Location: Street/Box # _____ On _____ Side of _____

between _____ and _____

in _____ Subdivision _____ County

ID by _____

Date Construction to Begin _____

Contractor _____ Loan Officer _____

	Percentage of Construction				
1. Start-up costs	1				
2. Rough clearing and grading	1				
3. Foundations	4				
4. Floor framing	4				
5. Wall framing	5				
6. Roof framing and sheeting	5				
7. Wall sheathing	1				
8. Roofing	2				
9. Well/water connection	2				
10. Septic tank/sewer tap	2				
11. Plumbing roughed	5				
12. Wiring roughed	3				
13. Heating-AC ducts	2				
14. Insulation	2				
15. Chimney/flue	2				
16. Siding/brick veneer	7				
17. Door frames set	2		27. Cabinets	3	
			28. Heat plant	2	
18. Windows set	3		29. Exterior painting	2	
19. Particle board/flooring	2		30. Interior painting	4	
20. Inside walls	6		31. Built-in appliances	2	
21. Bath tile	2		32. Electrical fixtures	2	
22. Outside trim	2		33. Carpet/floor finish	4	
23. Gutters	1		34. Screens	1	
24. Inside trim	3		35. Drives and walks	3	
25. Doors hung	2		36. Cleaning	1	
26. Plumbing fixtures	4		37. Landscaping	1	

TOTAL	100%
DATE	
INSPECTOR	
INSPECTOR	

There is a considerable time period during construction in which the house progresses toward completion, but you haven't received bills for materials. It will take you approximately six months to complete the house, and because of the billing time lag from suppliers and loan interest being one month or more in arrears, in that six months you will have had an average of only 40 percent of the total money available disbursed to you. This is an approximate figure, obviously, as is the time frame needed to complete your house. I'm merely pointing out that you won't pay interest on the full amount of your mortgage until the house is complete. At that time the lender will complete the disbursement of the construction money and convert the loan to a permanent mortgage for twenty to thirty years. Then you will be making your full payments of principal and interest. But then you have your dream house. Move in. If that sounds simple, it is only because it is.

Two Houses?

By the way, even in a sluggish market, houses sell sooner or later. If you already have a home and you fear it won't sell before your new one is ready, either don't worry about it or sell it first and live in an apartment while building your new home.

The other financing charges will vary with lenders and attorneys, but can be estimated in advance. They will total about 2–3 percent of the mortgage amount. They may have to be paid when you close your construction loan, or they may be deducted from the mortgage.

I prefer the latter method. It doesn't tie up my cash. They also are a construction cost.

Cash Needed

You will need some extra cash. Call it interim or short-term financing. Some expenses will occur before your lender makes the first disbursement of construction money and you will need a few thousand dollars to bridge that gap for such things as paying subs, fees, and permits. If you have cash available, fine. If not, you may want to borrow from a commercial bank or take a second mortgage on your existing home, or a *bridge loan*.

Excluding the cost of the land and the 2–3 percent we discussed, you shouldn't need more than an additional 5 percent of the cost of the house for interim operating expenses. This money is needed only until the house is finished. When the lender disburses all the money in the form of the permanent loan, the need for your operating cash will disappear and you can put it back where you got it.

If it is borrowed, include the interest paid in your cost estimate. It, too, is a cost of construction that other builders and I have included. It may seem that I put the cart before the horse by discussing interest charges first, but many worry about them and I want to allay that worry.

FHA and VA loans are government-backed and they deal **only** with permanent financing and not construction financing. Your local lender will coordinate the construction loan.

Usually the lenders will require that your land be paid for in full and that you have a *clear title* to it before they will lend you money to build on it. This is to protect them. Quite simply put, if you don't have clear title to the land, they won't have clear title to their *note* to you for construction money.

There is a whole profession handling those matters, so we won't go further into them than that. Your attorney can explain the legalese far better. It is not necessary for you to become versed in law to be your own general contractor.

Lot Subordination

There is a way to avoid paying for the land before construction. It is called *lot subordination*. It means the owner will take a note in lieu of payment of all or part of the asking price, and legally subordinate his or her interest in that land to your lender. Consult your attorney for details. Some lenders won't allow this or any other form of borrowing for the land or down payment. Usually the land is the down payment as its value is close to the normal dollar amount put down on a house. Lenders want that money to be your *equity*. They may have you sign a statement that you aren't borrowing your down payment.

But in your case, you are saving an amount equal to your down payment or your land by being your own builder. The builder's profit and overhead you are saving is a legitimate figure. You will earn it and it will be an actual dollar amount when the house is finished.

Lenders will have different opinions of many of your particular financing needs. You will need to shop around and spend some time talking to them. They will help you tremendously in putting your financial package together. In this aspect, they are like a subcontractor. All will also explain their policies on construction draws, inspections, construction loan interest payments, points, credit reports, qualifications, and interest rates.

A CHOICE OF MORTGAGES

Here are some of the mortgages being issued today:

Conventional mortgage. My favorite because it involves the least amount of red tape, and usually is fastest to get. You may have to have a larger down payment, depending on the laws in your state, and the requirements of the lender.

Federal Housing Administration Mortgage. FHA insures the loan. The down payments required are small, the repayment period is up to thirty-five years, but it may take time for you to get your loan approved and for FHA to check out your plans. Your lender will have specific details.

Veterans Administration Mortgage. You have to qualify as a veteran to get the VA to guarantee your loan. No down payment is required in some cases. Approval is sometimes slow. Ask your lender for specific details.

Farmers Home Administration Mortgage. There are both guaranteed mortgages and loans made directly from FmHA funds. The interest rate you pay depends on your family income and the size of your family. This can be an excellent way to borrow for a low-income family. Check this one by telephoning the FmHA, listed in your telephone directory under U.S. Government, Agriculture Department.

The high interest rates of the late 70s and early 80s sparked interest in new ways of financing homes. We'll mention a few of these, and will promise that there will be more that you might want to investigate.

The most simple is the *mortgage financed by the seller.* Used more often for home sales than for lot sales, this mortgage has terms negotiated by the two parties involved.

The *graduated payment mortgage* is tailored for young people with expectations of higher incomes. Monthly payments are small at first, but gradually increase. Figure out total payments under this mortgage, and compare them with those of a conventional mortgage before being swayed by those smaller early monthly payments.

The *variable-rate mortgage* can be written so that monthly payments or the total number of those payments can be changed during the life of the mortgage as interest rates move up or down.

The Permanent Mortgage

Qualifying for a Loan

As to qualifications or "qualifying for a loan," the requirements change daily and are different for each lender. A rule of thumb that is often bent is that your annual mortgage payments (only on your permanent mortgage) should not exceed 2–2½ times your gross monthly income from **all** sources. Local lenders will have various rules of thumb, but most will be about like this. Also, the more money you put down (increasing your equity), the more willing a lender will be to lend you money, and often at a lower interest rate.

Don't forget, the thousands of dollars you are saving activing as general contractor are a legitimate value, and are to be, under all circumstances, considered as cash equity.

Keep this in mind when talking to lenders: due to more and more people being squeezed out of the housing market each day by high prices and interest rates, lenders are making fewer loans. Yet they must make loans to stay in business. It is a major source of their income. Perhaps you might have been squeezed out, too, in the past, but now, by being your own general contractor, you can handle a loan.

How Big a Mortgage?

How much house you need and therefore how much you need to borrow is up to you. Chapter 4 offers a fast, easy, and fairly accurate method of estimating the costs. Stretching your budget for more house is not all bad, because:

1. You get a house large enough for a growing family.
2. You are making a good investment. Houses appreciate in value while you get an excellent tax write-off on the tax-deductible interest.
3. Your income will probably catch up in a few years. Check into graduated mortgage payments or variable interest rates.
4. You can always bail out by selling the completed house and recoup all costs plus a profit. Then you're ready, of course, to reinvest in another new home.

Financing may be the most difficult phase of construction as it will be the one in which you may feel the least adequate. You will find, however, that after talking to one or two lenders, you'll be more relaxed and better versed in their jargon. Of course, you may get lucky and establish a good relationship with the first one you approach.

CHAPTER 4

Cost Estimating

ESTIMATING THE COST of building a house is not an exact science. You can, however, come reasonably close to estimating a total cost, and you can guide the total project toward that estimated total. For precise estimating, draw up an estimate sheet like the one in this chapter, and fill in each item based on the square footage of the house you are going to build, or on actual bids from subcontractors.

The next to last column on the estimating sheet, labeled *estimated cost,* is designed for speed in arriving at a fairly accurate estimate of what you can afford and for preparing your estimate for the lender. It probably won't differ more than 5 percent from the actual costs. The *actual cost* column is for entering paid bills. This column will be accurate because it will be filled in when each category is completed and has been paid for.

Most lumber companies will do a take-off (estimate) of the materials they hope to sell you. For your first house I'd advise you to let them. That doesn't mean you have to buy from them. More on this in Chapter 7. Your carpenter can also do a take-off of materials he will use. He may or may not charge for this service. Ask him.

As you pay for items during construction, compare them to your original estimate so you can see how the cost is running. If costs run higher than estimated in some categories, you may want to trim some costs in others.

Most of the heavy costs come at the beginning of construction, for such items as lumber, masonry, carpentry, plumbing, electrical work, and heating plants. Some of

the items bought later are still quite significant in affecting the total cost of the house. These include carpeting, appliances, bath accessories, wallpapering (which can be postponed, to save money), parquet floors and other flooring, and special *moldings.* It is possible to cut costs on these.

I have seen houses with thousands of dollars worth of molding just on the first floor. Molding can be added later if reducing costs is important. Windows can vary because of brand name, and the difference in quality is negligible. Do you need a ten-cycle dishwasher, when a five-cycle or a two-cycle will do as well? So it is with each item.

Balancing Costs

As you prepare your estimate using the form in this chapter, you will find single item costs varying greatly.

Why would a single item vary so much? For three reasons:

1. Prices of materials vary daily — sometimes substantially.
2. Different tradesmen use different amounts of materials. Some carpenters overbuild and will use more lumber to do the same job as someone else. (Let them. I'd rather overbuild in framing than underbuild.) This is just one house, and you can save somewhere else. If you were building ten to fifty houses a year, you would need to be more careful with materials used.

3. It is impossible to determine the exact number of *studs*, *joists*, bricks, and other materials that go into a house. Some estimators are more accurate than others, but an exact estimate is pure luck.

Don't worry yourself to death over the lack of exactness. A builder pads an estimate by at least 5 percent to cover these contingencies. That is just one reason why you'll be saving by being your own general contractor. Don't worry about that lack of exactness, but keep an eye on each category as you get bids and prices.

The number of bricks and concrete blocks required is the most difficult to estimate. Brick companies often will estimate for you, but they won't be any more accurate than you on your first try.

You have a choice of making a rough estimate and ordering from it, or having the brick company do it. If you don't have enough bricks, you can order more. If you order too many, you can return the surplus. (Ask the brick company about its return policy when you're shopping for your brick.) Or, quite often, your masonry sub will buy unused brick at a discounted price and haul them off the job for you. Ordering bricks may be the most difficult part of estimating — but only if you let it bother you. I recommend ordering a little short and letting the brick company hold some extra bricks in its brickyard in your name so that if you need to order more, you'll get the same *color run*.

You'll need about five to seven bags of mortar cement per 1,000 bricks. Sand is ordered in such enormous quantities — fourteen or sixteen cubic yards — that you don't have to concern yourself with exactness. If I seem to oversimplify a very complex item — good. Don't worry about it. Order a little less than you think you need of sand, brick, and block, and if you run out, order more. Your masonry sub will be sure to let you know in advance if he is going to run short of an item, because if he doesn't he will be held up.

Many masonry subs can estimate needs. If you find one who does, let him. Some even supply their own materials — better yet.

Never be too proud to ask questions, from either a supplier or subcontractor. Both are very willing to help. They don't make any money until they sell you something or perform a service. Also, some plans purchased in magazines come with or make available for a fee a schedule of materials, right down to the amount of nails. They are fairly accurate. I wouldn't hesitate to use them. Suppliers also do this free. See Chapter 7.

ESTIMATING BRICKS NEEDED

To figure the area of a wall, multiply the length times the width (or the base times the height). If the wall is to be eight feet high and the base is twenty feet long, the area is 160 square feet.

If you plan a brick foundation one *course* in thickness, which is what you would have on a house with a relatively low crawl space, here is how to determine how many standard 2″ x 4″ x 8″ bricks you would need.

The foundation is 30′ x 60′ x 3′. Treat each wall as a separate area, determine that area, add all areas together, and multiply by eight. Multiplying by eight is generous because it requires 7.5 bricks plus mortar space per square foot of surface area:

So our 30′ x 60′ x 3′ foundation would use the following:

Side 1	30 x 3 =	90 square feet
Side 2	60 x 3 =	180 square feet
Side 3	30 x 3 =	90 square feet
Side 4	60 x 3 =	180 square feet
Total		540 square feet x 8 = 4,320 bricks

COST BREAKDOWNS

Now we'll cover each item or category on the estimating sheet, and give the easiest way to get an estimated cost. On some you'll be able to get an actual cost before you start; on some you won't.

Estimate of Construction Costs

	Cost Per Square Foot	Estimated Cost	Actual Cost
1. Loan closing costs ....$	$	$	
2. Construction loan interest ....$	$	$	
3. Builders' risk (fire) insurance..........$	$	$	
4. Temporary utilities ....$	$	$	
5. Plans and specifications ....$	$	$	
6. Start-up costs ....$	$	$	
7. Clearing and grading ....$	$	$	
8. Excavation (minimal with crawl space)...$	$	$	
9. Footings ....$	$	$	
10. Foundation........................$	$	$	
11. Waterproofing foundation.............$	$	$	
12. Framing lumber and materials ....$	$	$	
13. Framing labor ....$	$	$	
14. Steel ....$	$	$	
15. Windows ....$	$	$	
16. Exterior doors ....$	$	$	
17. Roofing..........................$	$	$	
18. Concrete slab actual area ....$	$	$	
19. Exterior trim, materials ....$	$	$	
20. Exterior trim, labor..................$	$	$	
21. Brick veneer and fireplace — See text for other siding ....$	$	$	
22. Plumbing ....$	$	$	
23. Heating, air conditioning, and vents .....$	$	$	
24. Electrical.........................$	$	$	
25. Insulation ....$	$	$	
26. Water and sewer ....$	$	$	
27. Drywall..........................$	$	$	
28. Cabinets ....$	$	$	
29. Interior trim.......................$	$	$	
30. Interior doors ....$	$	$	
31. Interior trim, labor ....$	$	$	
32. Painting..........................$	$	$	
33. Appliances ....$	$	$	
34. Light fixtures ....$	$	$	
35. Flooring ....$	$	$	
36. Driveway, walks, patio ....$	$	$	
37. Cleaning ....$	$	$	
38. Gutters, screens ....$	$	$	
39. Wallpaper ....$	$	$	
40. Hardware and bath accessories ....$	$	$	
41. Landscape........................$	$	$	
42. Miscellaneous (allow 3%) ....$	$	$	

TOTAL COST = $ or $ per square foot of heated area.

To estimate garages, the following numbered items should be calculated per square foot of garage area in addition to the amount calculated for heated area: 1, 2, 3, 8, 9, 10, 11, 12, 13, 14, 15, 16, 17, 18, 19, 20, 21, 32, 38.

To estimate an unfinished basement, the following numbered items should be calculated per square foot of basement area, in addition to any amounts calculated for heated area or garage area: 1. 2, 3, 5, 8, 10, 11, 14, 18.

For finishing the basement, add the appropriate numbered items for each degree of finishing you desire.

For each year subsequent, allow a percent increase per item for inflation.

1. Loan closing costs. These costs consist of charges made by the lender, your attorney's fees for preparing the paperwork and certifying *clear title* to the land, *title insurance,* if required, prepaid insurance and taxes, credit reports, *recording fees,* and any other charges necessary to make your loan to construct your house, and to provide permanent financing (20–30 years). The fees generally total a percentage of the loan amount. They will therefore vary with the size of the house.

2. Construction loan interest. This is interest charged by the lender for the money advanced to you to pay your suppliers and subs during construction. It is a cost of construction and is therefor paid out of construction money, as explained in Chapter 3. You are only charged interest on the amount you've actually taken out at any given time and therefore the amount of interest will increase as the house progresses and you draw out construction funds to pay for labor and materials. You are only paying interest, no principal.

When the house is finished and all funds are disbursed by the lender, the loan will be converted to a permanent mortgage. Then you will be paying principal and interest on the total amount borrowed. (You will know the amount beforehand as the lending institution will discuss this with you when you apply for a loan and when it helps you determine how much of a loan you can afford.)

3. Builders' risk insurance, liability insurance. Builders' risk or fire insurance covers the dwelling in case it burns or is damaged. Lending institutions require this to protect them. It also protects you in case the house burns before it is finished. This policy does not cover personal possessions, so don't put any in the house before moving in unless you arrange a satisfactory agreement with the insurance company.

When you move in, you will be covered by your homeowners' policy (which will also be required by the lender), but that policy is not a cost of construction. Fire insurance is not expensive and the cost will vary by company and locale.

You may also want to carry, and may be required to carry, liability insurance in case someone is injured on the job site. Workers will be covered by the liability insurance of the subs, as discussed in Chapter 6. Your insurance is inexpensive.

4. Temporary utilities. These consist of water and electricity that you will need to construct the house. Obtaining them is covered in Chapter 7.

5. Plans and specifications. These costs will vary considerably, as discussed in Chapter 2.

6. Start-up costs. Your building permit, surveys, lot staking, and miscellaneous costs.

7. Clearing and grading the lot, plus hauling debris away. Again, this will vary depending upon such factors as locale, terrain, weather at the time, and soil.

8. Excavation for basement. Will vary for the same reasons as number 7.

9. Footings. Will vary for the same reasons as numbers 7 and 8.

10. Foundation. This item will vary more than any other. A steeply sloping lot will use much more materials than a flat lot if there is no basement. A basement house will use more than a non-basement house; a house built on a slab even less than both the others.

11. Waterproofing foundation. Use professionals; names listed in the Yellow Pages.

12. Framing lumber and materials. A list on page 40 gives you an idea of what goes into the "framing package," as it is called. It includes all materials except windows, doors, and roofing shingles (although it can include those) that are necessary to *dry-in the house.* The take-off in the Appendix was done by my carpenters and was free.

13. Framing labor. This is the labor required to bring the house to the dried-in stage. After this stage is complete, all other stages can commence, some simultaneously. The only way to contract for this job is by the square foot with the square footage agreed to before you start. Five people will arrive at five different square footage totals, using the same set of plans. Some will vary by 300 or more square feet. Sounds incredible, doesn't it? But I swear it's true. In determining square footage, houses are measured from outside wall to outside wall, not from roof overhangs. If the house is not easily divided into rectangles for simplifying square footage determination, and you can't figure it out, have the designer do it for you. Ready-made plans generally come with the square footage broken down for you. Use those figures. Have an agreement on attic space.

14. Steel requirements and usage. These are determined by design and should be indicated on the plans. You should not even have to concern yourself with this matter other than ordering the necessary pieces from a steel company. They will do the take-off, if needed, free of charge.

Most houses, except those with basements, require little if any steel. Openings in load-bearing walls greater than eight feet should have steel above them. Wood beams spanning larger distances will sag after a period of time. Steel is usually cheaper and always better. Your carpenters will know how to install various pieces of steel, so don't worry about it. Only in cases of large heavy I beams (very rarely used) will a crane service be necessary. If a crane is needed, it is no big deal and really not that expensive.

I remember the first time I had to use one. I was petrified; I thought I was really getting in over my head. The crane arrived, set the beams, two over a basement, and was gone — all within sixty minutes. The beams weighed close to 1,000 pounds each and it would have taken ten men two to three hours to do the same amount of work, if they could have done it at all. Steel costs vary considerably; but for the traditional house you will generally need steel only in the garage area.

15. Windows. This cost is simple to estimate since you have an exact count. I do not recommend any particular brand, but I do recommend that you visit a couple of building supply companies and compare. Most carry more than one brand. Locally made windows usually are less expensive than national brands and give as good a warranty service. For special windows such as angular or bay windows get exact quotes from the supplier. Generally there is no additional cost to install windows (except special or unusual ones) as that labor is included in your carpenter's framing charge. Be sure it is.

16. Exterior doors. They are as easy to estimate as windows, and all that was said for windows applies, including the labor to install being included in the framing bill from your carpenter. Sliding glass doors may require a separate installation charge; that depends on your carpenter. Be sure to ask whoever installs sliding glass doors to caulk under the threshold thoroughly, preferably with silicone type caulking.

17. Roofing. It is measured and estimated by squares. A square of roofing is ten feet square or 100 square feet. The number of squares can be determined by your supplier, your carpenter, or you. I advise either of the first two for your first house. They won't be exact, but may come a little closer than you will. Shingles are priced by their weight per square and the material from which they are made. Generally we are talking about either asphalt or fiberglass and their weight per square is from 245 pounds to 345 pounds. Also there are cedar shakes and slate, tin, tar and gravel (built-up roofs). But in this book we will deal with asphalt and fiberglass. The cost of labor to install will depend upon the sub, the weight of the shingle, and the pitch of the roof — the steeper the pitch the higher the price for labor. The same applies to weight. The heavier they are, the higher the price. Most roofs are the 245-pound asphalt variety and

most roof pitches average about six inches for each foot of horizontal travel (a 6/12 pitch).

18. Concrete flatwork (slabs), garage floors, basement floors. This refers to smooth finish concrete work, not rough finish as in driveways, patios, and walks. It also involves the use of other materials such as Styrofoam, wire mesh, *expansion points* and *polyurethane*. Your concrete subcontractor can explain this to you. The work is closely inspected by most building departments.

19. Exterior trim materials. These are the materials used to trim around the roof line, *soffitt, fascia board, soffit vents*, moldings, posts, and *drip caps*. Materials vary with the type of house.

20. Exterior trim, labor.

21. Brick veneer. This will include all materials and labor in addition to exterior trim and labor. Include for fireplace and chimney.

21A. Cedar siding. Labor should be included under #20.

21B. Masonite siding. Labor should be included under #20.

22. Plumbing. Includes all fixtures such as water closets, faucets, sinks, and water heater. Does not include dishwasher, disposal, washing machine, or ice maker.

23. Heating and air-conditioning, using *heat pump*. Includes venting of bathrooms, stove hoods, and dryers.

24. Electrical. Includes all switches, receptacles, wires, *panels, breakers*, wiring of all built-in appliances, and careful compliance with codes. All copper except heavy wire pulled to large appliances and panel boxes where aluminum may be used safely.

25. Insulation. Includes all wall, floor, ceiling requirements to meet R-13, R-19, R-30 respectively. These figures are measures of the efficiency of the insulation. Other areas of the country may require more or less insulation to meet energy standards. Consult with your utilities as to whether lower rates are offered if their insulation specifications are met.

26. Water and sewer hookup charges. In a city, with services offered, or for well and septic tank in country.

27. Drywall. (½" x 4' x 12'). Labor and materials to hang, tape joints, finish (two coats).

28. Cabinets. Includes kitchen cabinets and bathroom vanity cabinets. Exact bid may be figured by supplier from plans.

29. Interior trim. Includes all moldings, closet shelves, and stairway trim; also includes *carpet underlayment*.

30. Interior doors. Solid six-panel wood doors; one-half for hollow doors.

31. Interior trim labor. To install all materials in #29 and #30, and door hardware.

32 Painting. Interior and exterior and all materials.

33. Appliances. Built-in only, that is dishwasher, disposal, stove. No washing machine, dryer, or refrigerator. Will vary with the quality.

34. Light fixtures. Includes door bells, bath fans, and an average number of light fixtures.

35. Flooring. Will vary considerably as to type, wood, carpet, tile, etc.

36. Driveways, walks, patios. Will vary considerably as to material (concrete, asphalt, stone, brick) and length of each.

37. Cleaning. Inside and outside trash, windows, baths, top to bottom inside.

38. Gutters, screens.

39. Wallpaper. Will vary considerably.

40. Hardware. Includes doorknobs, locks, deadbolts, and toilet tissue holders.

41 Landscape.

42 Miscellaneous. Allow 3% of total cost for unforeseen costs and cost increases.

CHAPTER 5

Further Preparations

YOU HAVE PURCHASED a lot, selected house plans, estimated costs, and arranged your construction loan and permanent mortgage. Several details still need your attention before you break ground.

Obtain a building code book or pamphlet from your local building inspector, listed in the phone book. If you don't have a building inspection department, and many small towns don't, find out about any local or state codes, and how they are enforced. This information can be obtained through City Hall, the Town Hall, your lender, or an attorney. You need not be an expert on codes, but it is best to be familiar with a few of the important specifications, such as those that relate to the thickness of footings, the preparation of concrete slabs, and requirements for foundation walls and lumber spans. If you don't have a building inspection department, a local library should have a code book for your state and/or county, and several good reference books on each trade involved in the construction business. You may want to do this before getting a loan. Regulations could change your plans and increase your costs.

Again, I emphasize that you need not be an expert. Your subs will know, or should know, the codes as they apply to their particular fields. If there is a question, you'll know where to find the correct answer if you have a code book and reference books. If you find good subs, you may never use those references.

Also, at this point, you must find out the procedure for obtaining your building permit. This can be done over the phone to the building inspection department. Officials will also tell you the procedures for inspections such as when to call for them, and which phases of construction require inspection. Good subcontractors will have this information and take care of the inspections for you.

Inspections Required

As an example, my county requires the following inspections:

1. Temporary electrical, or *saw service*, to insure proper grounding.

2. Footing, before pouring concrete, to make sure we have reached solid load-bearing ground.

3. Slab, before concrete is poured, to determine if it is properly insulated. Any plumbing in the slab is also inspected at this time.

4. Electrical, plumbing, heating, and air-conditioning rough-in, to insure that in-the-wall installations that can't be seen later are correct.

5. Framing rough-in, to insure structural integrity, especially after electrical, plumbing, heating, and air-conditioning installations. These workers have been known to cut too deeply into a joist or stud and weaken it.

6. Insulation, to insure compliance with new local standards.

7. Final electrical, plumbing, heating, air-conditioning, and building to insure they work properly, comply with codes, and are safe. All final inspections must be completed before we can get more than temporary electrical service.

BUILDING PERMIT DEPARTMENT OF BUILDINGS AND SAFETY ENGINEERING

PERMIT NO.

THE BUREAU OF LICENSES AND PERMITS   DATE   19
HEREBY GRANTS PERMISSION TO

NAME   ADDRESS   CONTRACTOR'S
STATE LICENSE

TO   (   ) STORY   NUMBER OF
APARTMENTS

ON THE   SIDE OF (BUILDING NO.)   ST. OR   ZONING
AVE.   DISTRICT

BETWEEN   AND   ST. OR
AVE.

LOT NO. AND
SUBDIVISION   SIZE

BUILDING IS TO BE   FT. WIDE BY   FT. LONG BY   FT. IN HEIGHT
AND SHALL CONFORM IN CONSTRUCTION TO TYPE

USE GROUP   BASEMENT WALLS OR FOUNDATION

REMARKS:

APPROVED BY

1

CUBIC FEET   ESTIMATED COST $ REGULAR FEE $

ZONING FEE $

OWNER   BUREAU OF LICENSES AND PERMITS

ADDRESS   BY

THIS PERMIT CONVEYS NO RIGHT TO OCCUPY ANY STREET, ALLEY OR SIDEWALK OR ANY PART THEREOF, EITHER TEMPORARILY OR PERMANENTLY. ENCROACHMENTS ON PUBLIC PROPERTY, NOT SPECIFICALLY PERMITTED UNDER THE BUILDING CODE, MUST BE APPROVED BY THE COMMON COUNCIL. STREET OR ALLEY GRADES AS WELL AS DEPTH AND LOCATION OF PUBLIC SEWERS MAY BE OBTAINED FROM THE DEPARTMENT OF PUBLIC WORKS – CITY ENGINEERS OFFICE. THE ISSUANCE OF THIS PERMIT DOES NOT RELEASE THE APPLICANT FROM THE CONDITIONS OF ANY APPLICABLE SUBDIVISION RESTRICTIONS.

MINIMUM OF THREE CALL INSPECTIONS REQUIRED FOR ALL CONSTRUCTION WORK:
1. FOUNDATIONS OR FOOTINGS.
2. PRIOR TO COVERING STRUCTURAL MEMBERS (READY TO LATH).
3. FINAL INSPECTION FOR COMPLIANCE PRIOR TO OBTAINING CERTIFICATE OF OCCUPANCY.

APPROVED PLANS MUST BE RETAINED ON JOB AND THIS CARD KEPT POSTED UNTIL FINAL INSPECTION HAS BEEN MADE. WHERE A CERTIFICATE OF OCCUPANCY IS REQUIRED, SUCH BUILDING SHALL NOT BE OCCUPIED UNTIL FINAL INSPECTION HAS BEEN MADE AND CERTIFICATE OBTAINED.

SEPARATE PERMITS REQUIRED FOR ELECTRICAL AND PLUMBING INSTALLATIONS

POST THIS CARD

Continued on page 27

BUILDING PERMIT continued

BUILDING INSPECTION APPROVALS	PLUMBING INSPECTION APPROVALS

BUILDING INSPECTION APPROVALS

1
DRAIN TILE AND
FOUNDATION _____

DATE_____

INSPECTOR_____

2
SUPERSTRUCTURE _____
(PRIOR TO LATH AND PLASTER)

DATE_____

INSPECTOR_____

3
FINAL INSPECTION_____

DATE_____

INSPECTOR_____

> WORK SHALL NOT PROCEED UNTIL EACH
> BUREAU HAS APPROVED THE VARIOUS
> STAGES OF CONSTRUCTION.

PLUMBING INSPECTION APPROVALS

1
BUILDING SEWER
(A) SANITARY _____

DATE _____ INSPECTOR _____

(B) STORM _____

DATE _____ INSPECTOR _____

2
CROCK TO IRON _____

DATE _____ INSPECTOR _____

3
UNDERGROUND STORM DRAINS _____

DATE _____ INSPECTOR _____

4
ROUGH PLUMBING _____

DATE _____ INSPECTOR _____

5 WATER PIPING
INAL INSPECTION _____

DATE _____ INSPECTOR _____

ELECTRICAL INSPECTION APPROVALS

1
ROUGHING IN _____

DATE_____

INSPECTOR_____

2
FINAL INSPECTION _____

DATE_____

INSPECTOR_____

SAFETY ENGINEERING APPROVAL

3
APPROVED _____

DATE_____

INSPECTOR_____

> INSPECTIONS INDICATED ON THIS CARD
> CAN BE ARRANGED FOR BY TELEPHONE
> OR WRITTEN NOTIFICATION.

You can now select materials such as brick, shingles, windows, doors, roofing, trim, plumbing, fixtures, built-in appliances, light fixtures, flooring, hardware, and wallpaper. As you visit building supply houses to see their samples, you can also take care of a couple of other large items:

1. Open your line of credit with them. This is quite easy, even for an inexperienced builder. See Chapter 7 on suppliers.

2. Ask them to recommend reliable subcontractors. Smaller building supply companies are better equipped to furnish this information because the management is more directly involved with customers. The key sub you are looking for is your carpenter, and most of the good ones patronize building supply houses from time to time. Many make building supply houses their source of referrals. This is especially true in resort areas. (Don't forget, you can also use this book as a guide to building a second home in a resort area.) You may find other subs here. More in the next chapter about subs.

Now is the time to contact your gas, electric, and water departments for hookup procedures. Every locale has different utilities and thus different procedures. If you so desire, you will also want to order a *prewire* from your phone company at this time as the company sometimes requires three to five weeks' notice. Some don't charge for this, some do. Ask first.

You will also want to shop around for a builder's risk or fire policy from various insurance agents. In most states, they are fairly equal in policy, being governed by state laws. Be sure to check. The policy should take effect when materials arrive on the job but your lender may want it to be in force before it closes the construction loan. The lender will be the payee in the policy since it is the company's money. When the house is complete, and you move in, the fire policy can be converted to homeowners' insurance, often at a fairly good savings over a new homeowners' policy.

Doing Your Own Labor

If you plan to do any of your own labor, I have only one thing to say — if you aren't an expert at the particular trade you plan to do yourself, forget it. It'll end up costing you more in time and money than you will save. This is especially true in painting. People think it is so easy, but unfortunately it comes at a time when the house is quite far along, and construction disbursements will be approaching their maximum amount. You need painters who can get it and get out, do the job fast, and at the same time do a respectable job. If you seek perfection in painting, wait until you are living in the house and do your own touch-up painting.

If you hire painters by the hour, plan to stay with them the whole time, or else plan on it taking twice as long. You won't get a better job, or at least that much better, for the extra time. Hire them by a contract amount, so much a square foot based on heated area.

When it comes to doing your own work, remember one of Murphy's laws — "Nothing is as easy as it looks."

CHAPTER 6

Subcontractors

A SUBCONTRACTOR (SUB) is an individual or a firm that contracts to perform part or all of another contract. In your case you are technically the builder or general contractor, and you will build by subcontracting with others. You will pay for this by a predetermined contract amount with each one. This is important. You will have no hourly wage employees working for you. Thus you will avoid all of the governmental red tape and taxes concerning employees. Your subcontractors are not considered to be employees.

Your Subcontractors, Professionals

Here is a list of the subcontractors and professional people you probably will be contracting with, in the general order in which you will need them:

1. Attorney. Needed for initial assistance for questions, land purchase, loan assistance, *loan closing,* continuing assistance if necessary for legal questions and/or settling disputes with subs or suppliers. I would not attempt the project without an attorney. You can find one who specializes in real estate by calling the Lawyer's Referral Services (in the Yellow Pages) or a real estate company, or asking a friend. Attorney's fees are a cost of construction.
2. Lending officers at savings and loans, banks, or mortgage companies.
3. House designer or architect.
4. Carpentry sub, your key sub, to be lined up early.
5. Surveyor.
6. Grading and excavation contractor.
7. Footing contractor.
8. Brick masonry contractor. Builds the foundation.
9. Concrete (finisher) subcontractor. Pours the slab or concrete floor.
10. Waterproofing contractor.
11. Electrical contractor.
12. Plumbing contractor (and well and septic system, if needed).
13. Heating and air-conditioning and vent (HVAC) contractor.
14. Roofing contractor.
15. Insulation contractor.
16. Drywall contractor.
17. Painting contractor.
18. Flooring, carpet, and Formica contractor.
19. Tile contractor.
20. Cleaning crew contractor.
21. Landscape contractor.

Finding Your Subs

As mentioned earlier, a lumber supply store is the best place to start for finding your carpenter subcontractor. Your carpenter sub will be able to recommend almost everyone else, as he or she is on the job more than anyone else and knows most of the other subs involved in building a house.

"A good sub is a working sub," especially during a recession. This is not always true, but is a pretty safe bet. The really good ones are sought after and in demand because they do good work and are reliable.

If you can't find a sub through a supplier or your carpenter, the next best place to look is on a job. Find a house under construction. Stop and ask around. You can get names, prices, and references. This takes only a few minutes. It is done all the time and the general contractor shouldn't mind.

Often the boss or owner of a subcontracting firm is on the job. Get his or her number and arrange a meeting. Sometimes there are signs at the job site advertising different subs.

Subs of only certain trades are listed in the Yellow Pages. Carpenters and most independent brick masons are not listed. You'll probably find heating and air-conditioning companies, plumbers, electricians, roofers, waterproofing companies, lumber dealers, and appliance manufacturers. Lumber dealers are a good source for names of carpenters and other trades.

CARPENTRY LABOR CONTRACT

To: (your name) _____   Sub cont. _____

   (address) _____   _____

             _____

Date: _____   Job address: _____

                                         _____

Owner: _____

Area: Heated _____ sq. ft.
               Unheated _____ sq. ft.
               Decks _____ sq. ft.

CHARGES

Framing   @ _____ sq.ft. x _____ sq.ft.=$_____

Boxing and

     siding   @ _____ sq.ft. x _____ sq.ft.=$_____

Interior trim   @ _____ sq.ft. x _____ sq.ft.=$_____

Decks   @ _____ sq.ft. x _____ sq.ft.=$_____

Setting

    Fireplace $_____

Setting

    Cabinets $_____

Paneling $_____

Misc. $_____

                           TOTAL CHARGES $_____

Signed: (your name) _____

    Date: _____

Signed: (subcontractor) _____

    Date: _____

Each subcontractor should carry insurance on his or her employees, and should provide you with a certificate of insurance. (See example in Appendix.)

It should not be a problem if most subs in your area belong to unions. I state this because some people expect union labor to cost more or fear they will have to do excessive paperwork if they hire union members. Not so. Your subcontractor will be responsible for all compliances to the union and his or her prices should be competitive.

Since this is your first experience and you won't be familiar with prices in your area, get three or four bids, or quotes, before selecting a sub. Use a written contract with all subs.

SUBCONTRACTOR'S CONTRACT

Subcontractor: _____

   Address _____

Builder: _____

Date _____ Plan. No. _____

W. Comp. Ins. Co. & Agent _____

   Certificate No.: _____ Expiration Date: _____

Location of Work: _____

Total Price Per House: _____ ($..............) Dollars

Terms of Payment: _____

Work To Be Performed and Materials To Be Supplied:

FOR SUBCONTRACTOR: _____

Signature and Title

FOR BUILDER: _____

Signature and Title

   You may use the very simple ones I have provided or your attorney can provide you with one. Subcontractors may have their own contracts. At any rate, use one. Don't trust anyone's memory when it comes to dollars. Be sure your bids are comparable, that all are bidding on exactly the same work. If your specifications are properly spelled out in your plans, the bidding should be.

Bids for Plumbing

   Plumbing bids should include all plumbing fixtures right down to the toilet seat. They will not include accessories such as toilet paper holders. If colored fixtures are to be used, specify color and brand. Plumbing showrooms are your best bet for the selection of these fixtures. Magazines and brochures don't tell you enough, nor give prices. Most plumbing showrooms won't tell you the wholesale price, but you'll be paying list anyway, as the plumber makes a profit on each fixture and it's included in his bid. Don't make an issue of this. The small profit in the fixtures is one of the plumber's sources of income and he or she earns it.

   Your heating and air-conditioning contract should include vents, such as for the bath fan and clothes dryer, and stove and range hood vents. Electrical bids should include all switches, wiring, receptacles, circuit breakers, and their respective *panel boxes*, a temporary service box and installation, *saw service*, wiring of all built-in appliances, and installation of ovens and ranges, furnaces, heaters, and air-conditioners.

   All subcontractors should be responsible for obtaining inspections from the building department, but you will want to be sure they do or you will have to do it yourself. Lack of inspections can cause delays. Proceeding without getting inspections can be troublesome and expensive. If you, for example, put up drywall before having your wiring inspected, you could be made to tear down some of the drywall for the electrical inspector. This is not likely to happen, but the inspector could force the issue.

   Utilities must be connected. Exactly who is responsible for running water lines, sewer lines, and electrical hookups will vary with each subcontractor involved. Get the responsibility pinned down when you are hiring the subs, then follow through to be sure it is done properly.

Scheduling Your Subcontractors

   Try to schedule your subs to fit as best you can into the sequence of events outlined in Chapter 8. This won't always be possible, and one sub can hold up the process. This is why you should check their references. Reliability is as important as quality and in some cases more so.

Paying Your Subcontractors

When you sign your contract with your carpenter, you will agree on a contract price for the work. It is usually based on X number of dollars per square foot of heated area and X number of dollars per square foot of under roof, such as in the garage. Any decks are treated separately. Prices will vary with the area, unions, and the complexity of the job.

Never pay a sub for work not done, for work that is incomplete, or for an unsatisfactory job. Never pay in advance.

You should work out a schedule of payment with your carpenter. The carpenter and some of the other subs may require draws, or partial payments, as work progresses. This should be discussed before work begins. Don't be shy about it. They are accustomed to discussing such matters.

It is all right to pay a draw, but never pay more than for work done. If, for example, your carpenter says that framing is 50 percent finished, but has only completed the floor framing and wall framing, and hasn't finished the ceiling joists, roof framing, *sheathing* or *bridging*, it isn't 50 percent complete. It is nearer 40 percent complete.

Plumbers and electricians usually get 60 percent of the total contract price when their rough-in has been completed and inspected. Heating, vent, and air-conditioning rough-in payments depend upon the installation of equipment such as furnaces. If payment is just for duct work and some low voltage wiring, 20 percent of the total should suffice. If a furnace had to be installed during rough-in, add another 10 percent. Work out the arrangement with the sub before he or she starts. Subs almost always would like to get more money than they have in the job. Be sure there is enough money left in the total bid to complete the job if the HVAC dealer goes broke while you are still building. It has happened. You don't want to be stuck paying more to complete the job. You'll be covered better if you don't overpay on the rough-in.

Brick masons and painters are about the only other subs who will require a draw in progress. You will have to use your best judgment as to how much of the job is done. Again, don't get ahead of them in paying.

I seem to be saying the only way you'll get the job completed is if you owe your sub money. In some cases that is true, but in others it is only partially true. Some subs would finish regardless. The main objective is to get your job finished. Often subs will have more than one job going at one time. You want yours finished quickly and before one that was started after yours.

Make sure inspections by your country or city are completed and the work is approved before you make any payments at any phase of construction, other than partial draws. This is your assurance that the job will be done, and done properly.

Working with Subcontractors

If you get along well with people, you don't need to read the next few paragraphs. But if you have trouble, read them carefully. The fault — sometimes — may be yours.

At this point you've selected your subs. You're satisfied, now that you've checked them out, that they are honest, trustworthy, and experts in their fields.

Now let them work. Don't try to supervise every blow of a hammer, the placement of every stud. They know more about their trades than you do, and probably, if they came to you well recommended, they take pride in their work. Let them do it.

And, most emphatically, don't try to tell your subs their jobs, just because you have read this book and a few others. You'll get good work out of your subs if they understand you think they know their jobs, and you're depending on them for good advice and quality work.

CHAPTER 7

Suppliers

THE SUPPLIERS THAT you will be buying from are listed in this chapter by the type of products they sell. Some sell several different products and you can shorten your shopping time when you patronize them. All of them will require a credit check on you by means of the references that you give them. Usually three charge accounts and one bank reference are required. Your suppliers will also want the same of your lender. This lender reference is the key to your getting credit with them. Obviously, if your credit is strong enough for the lender, it's strong enough for the suppliers. Often, just the lender reference is enough.

The suppliers you most likely will be using are:

1. Sand and gravel company.
2. Brick company. For face (decorative) brick.
3. Concrete block and brick company. For mortar mix and the building blocks for foundations.
4. Concrete supply company. For concrete for basements, garages, footings, and driveways.
5. Lumber company. For framing lumber, nails, windows, doors, roofing, siding, paneling, and interior and exterior trim.
6. Floor covering company. For vinyl flooring, carpet, parquet flooring, and counter tops.
7. Lighting fixtures supply. For light fixtures, bathroom fans, exhaust fans. The firm will do a complete count of your lighting needs and help you stay within a dollar figure set during estimation.
8. Paint store. For wallpaper. Paint is usually purchased by your painter and included in the price per square foot.
9. Appliance store. Some lumber companies and lighting centers carry appliances.
10. Insulation company. For your insulation needs.
11. Tile company. For ceramic tile, marble, any decorative stonework.
12. Drywall company. For Sheetrock. Some lumber companies also sell Sheetrock.
13. Any other specialty type suppliers that you may need for certain items not carried by one of the above, such as cabinet shops. Most lumber companies sell cabinets.

An account at a plumbing supply company is not necessary because the plumber sub buys all these items. You may visit to make your selections.

Some of the suppliers listed may carry most of your needs. In some small towns I've seen lumber yards that carry everything from bricks to wallpaper. So long as their prices are competitive, that's fine.

This is my recommendation: when you find a lumber company, give your plans to the sales force and let them give you a list of all the items the company can provide and a complete cost list. I have never found a company that wouldn't do this. Some will do a complete take-off of all the lumber and other materials you will need. I have it done by a lumber company when I am pressed for time.

You will get a list of the number of studs, floor joists, windows, and rafters. It will be fairly accurate, so don't be afraid to use it. Remember, the company is eager to sell to you and this is part of its service. As the housing market gets slower, the company will become more eager. Company personnel can also explain different products to you and show you new products and ideas. Let all your suppliers aid you in take-offs and different product ideas.

Delivery of Materials

Most companies will also assist you in or be responsible for delivery, making certain the materials are delivered on time, but not days in advance so they may be stolen. This delivery system has worked particularly well for me when I have used one supplier for all framing and as much of the rest of the supplies as I could. In such a case I have permitted my carpenter to order needed materials from that supplier alone. The supplier has aided me in keeping an eye on the additional materials ordered.

Buying at Builders' Cost

"Ask and ye shall receive." If you don't you won't. Be sure to ask if the quoted price is the "builders' price." Tell the supplier that you are a builder, because you are. If you want to add "company" to your name (that is, Smith Company), fine. If it makes you feel better, do it. It costs nothing and it changes nothing legally (the credit will still be in your name). If you want to incorporate (form a corporation), talk to your attorney. I don't think you'll find it is necessary.

Paying Your Suppliers

Some suppliers offer at least thirty-day terms so that you pay the stated amount within that time without penalty. They also offer percentage discounts if your bill is paid by the tenth of the month following purchase. If you buy supplies on June 20, you must pay by July 10 to receive the discount. If you buy on June 1, you would still have until July 10 to pay and get the discount. I try not to order too much toward the end of the month and wait as much as a week, if I can, to get an extra thirty days to pay. Not all suppliers are as generous as this, and their terms will vary. Check with your suppliers on what terms will be offered you.

By getting favorable terms, and extra time in which to pay, you can be sure that your construction draw will cover the bill. You will also use construction draws to pay for all your supplies. You should never have to use any of your own money.

Construction draws are based on labor completed and materials in place, not stored or sitting on the job site. For example, if you order brick for the whole house (a *brick veneer* home) at the start of the job, you'll have to pay for the brick that's going to be used in the veneering before the lender advances the dollars for veneering. Instead, you should order the brick in two stages, first for the foundation, then for veneer when you're ready.

Bookkeeping

Bookkeeping is very simple when you are building only one house. Open a separate checking account to handle the construction of the house and pay all bills, no matter how small, by check. Code each check stub to one of the appropriate categories on the estimate sheet and record each amount on a sheet of paper until you have totalled all of the money spent on that category. Then enter the total amount in the actual cost column of the estimate sheet and compare the actual cost to the estimated cost.

You will want to record any sales tax paid for materials as this may be deductible from your personal income tax. The same is true for interest expenses and service charges from the lender. The sales tax for materials can be a substantial amount for you, as can the interest and service charges. Check with your accountant to verify the current state and federal tax regulations regarding deductions for sales tax on housing material, interest expenses, and service charges.

────────── CHAPTER 8 ──────────

Building the House

LOOK AT HOW much you have accomplished. You have
your building lot, you've arranged your loan, and you
have a house plan you can live with, and finance. You've
completed the vast amount of paperwork that includes
any necessary permits and insurance policies.

You have located most of your subs, and have contracts with them. You've visited various supply houses,
and worked out your accounts for bricks, concrete, and
lumber.

Congratulations. You've reached the day you thought
might never come. You're ready to start building.

What is the proper sequence of steps in building the
house, and how long will each take?

Let's make a list of them.

1. Staking the lot and house: 1–3 hours.
2. Clearing and excavation: 1–3 days.
3. Order utilities, temporary electric service, and a
   portable toilet: 1 hour.
4. Footings (steps 3 and 4 can be reversed). First
   inspection must be made *before* pouring: 1 day.
5. Foundation and soil treatment, then foundation
   survey: 1 week.
6. Rough-ins for plumbing, if on a slab, and inspection: 2–4 days.
7. Slabs, basement, and garage: 1–2 days.
8. Framing and drying-in: 1–3 weeks.
9. Exterior siding, trim, veneers: 1–3 weeks.
10. Chimney and roof shingles: 2 days–1 week.
11. Rough-ins, can be done while 9 and 10 are in
    progress: 1–2 weeks.
12. Insulation: 3 days.
13. Hardwood flooring and underlayment: 3 days–1
    week.
14. Drywall: 2 weeks.

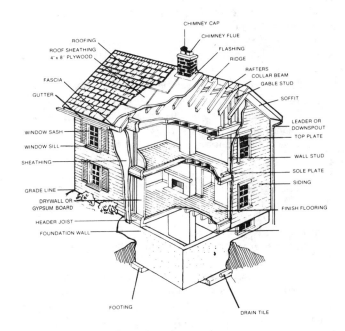

You can be a successful contractor of your own house without knowing a soffit
from a fascia, but it helps, in dealing with the subcontractors you hire, if you
can speak their language. You'll find in this illustration a sample of the common terms you'll hear used by your carpenters. For other terms of the trade,
and some you need to know when dealing with your home financing, see the
Glossary at the end of this book.

15. Prime walls and "point up": 2 days.
16. Interior trim and cabinets: 1–2 weeks.
17. Painting: 2–3 weeks.
18. Other trims, such as Formica, ceramic tile, vinyl
    floors: 1 day–1 week.
19. Trim out and finish plumbing, mechanical, elec-
    trical and hook up utilities: 1–2 weeks.
20. Clean up: 2–3 days.

35

21. Carpet and/or hardwood floor finish: 3 days–1 week.
22. Driveway (if concrete, can be poured anytime after 14): 1–3 days.
23. Landscaping: 1–3 days.
24. Final inspections, surveys, and closing of construction loan and interim loan: 1–3 days.
25. Enjoy: a lifetime.
(Note that steps 2 and 4 can be done by one sub.)

The Steps Explained

Let's take a closer look at those steps, and clear up any details you should know about them.

1. Staking the Lot and House (1–3 hours)

Since this will be, most likely, the first house you have built, I recommend that you have a registered surveyor/engineer do both. The least expensive one should be the one who surveyed the lot for purchase. Surveying is an important function as houses have been placed in violation of certain setbacks or restrictions, and if a surveyor does this, he or she is responsible. Builders have placed houses straddling property lines, and have had to tear the foundations out and start over. Best to be safe.

The stakes for the lot may have been moved or torn down since you purchased it. A surveyor will check this. Cost for restaking a lot and staking a house varies depending upon the complexity of the house and the terrain. You, of course, will want to be present for the staking or placing of the house to be certain it faces the direction that you want. You could meet with the surveyor early in the morning, at noon, or in the late afternoon, or even on a Saturday for this. Or you could put some stakes in the ground over a weekend, and thus indicate the approximate location and direction you desire. Then let the surveyor do it accurately and you can inspect it when it is done.

When the lot is cleared and the basement, if you have one, is dug, you may want the surveyor back to restake the house. On the first visit he or she usually will put in offset stakes. Offset stakes are the original four or two corners offset as much as twenty-five feet to the side so they won't be disturbed during clearing and excavation. Then it's a quick job to find the exact locations on the second visit.

Usually your house should face in the same direction as other houses on your side of the street. It doesn't have to, especially if your house is on a large lot, unless the building code demands this.

If your lot slopes more than three or four feet, you may need a *topographical plat*. Shop around among surveyors. You need it so that you can fit the house to the

slope, and be certain water will go around the house as it drains off the grade.

Water is, has been, and always will be the biggest problem that interferes with the construction of a building. It is nature's strongest force. It has shaped this planet. It will go where it can. It will take the shortest route. It is strong, stronger than anything people can make. Gutters help get rid of water. They don't control it. Keep it in mind.

The house should be positioned first on a map of your lot, then that position should be staked on the site by you and your carpenter, surveyor, or footing contractor. The surveyor is best. An architect or designer can position the house on the lot on paper, considering water as well as solar, wind, light, and the location of other houses. You should contribute your ideas to the person positioning the house. A few things to consider:

a. Light. A north-south facing house will be darker than an east-west facing house.

b. Water flow.

c. Other houses on the street.

d. The street it faces. Should the house be parallel with the street? What if the street curves? What about a corner lot?

e. Privacy, on the front, back, and sides.

f. The desire to use solar energy. Most solar homes have as much surface as possible facing south, with roof solar collectors or broad expanses of glass on that side, and a minimum of doors and windows on the north.

g. Minimum setback and side-yard requirements.

I don't want to frighten you with so many considerations. I have built many houses for my family, and I still have to think through these decisions. Positioning the house is a very personal decision, one you should make when you buy a lot. If you are stumped and you can't decide for yourself, and don't have an architect or designer involved with your plans, get the advice of an architect for that particular decision.

2. Clearing and Excavation (1–3 days)

Clearing the lot is what the title implies — clearing trees, brush, rocks, roots, and debris from where the house will sit, and usually ten feet around the site, thus allowing space for tractors, fork lifts, and trucks working at the site. Obviously, the more area to be cleared, the more it will cost. Big tree removal is time-consuming and expensive. Rocks may have to be blasted. If you want unwanted trees to be cut into firewood, the crew you hire will charge dearly for doing the job. Best to have the good, manageable-sized logs cut down to ten to twelve feet in length and piled at the side of the lot for you to cut up at your leisure.

Your best source for finding a sub for clearing and excavating is by word of mouth or in the Yellow Pages.

Get a *contract price* for this work. It may cost a little more, but you will be assured of not having your first cost overrun. If a basement is to be dug, your sub must have and know how to use a *transit*. You may also want your surveyor/engineer to oversee this digging to make certain it is the proper depth. Some or all of the dirt removed from the basement site might be put out of the way for later backfilling and landscaping. Topsoil should be separated, to be spread later for the lawn or garden.

Your contract price should include hauling all trash, such as stumps, branches, and rocks, to a suitable landfill. I don't advise burying trash on your lot as these stump holes tend to form an unsightly depression as the material in them settles or rots. Some areas ban stump holes. Of course, if the distance to a suitable landfill is prohibitively expensive and you have enough land, a stump hole may be your best choice.

You may want to put one or more loads of stone on your driveway so that supply trucks can drive in during wet weather. The best stone for this is unwashed crush stone. It has all the powdery substance created in crushing the stone, and this will harden after getting wet. You also may need to put drainpipes in at the roadside if they are required by either ordinance or common sense. They allow roadside water to flow under the driveway and prevent water from washing the stone away.

3. Utilities Hookup (1 hour)

When you purchased your lot, you were told (be sure you were) what utilities were available and how much they would cost. Now it's time to make plans for a couple of months down the road with a few phone calls and/or a visit to each utility. You should pay all fees and complete any necessary forms. Arrange for temporary electric service for your subs. Usually your electrician is responsible for installing the temporary electrical panel box and having it inspected, but **you** will have to apply for the service from the utility. This usually can be done over the phone.

Wells and *septic systems*, if used, can be installed now, and it is best to get this work done at this time. County or city health inspectors may be required by code to determine the location of these. Tell them your plans for such things as gardens or driveways, or which trees you hope to save, to guide them in their decisions.

If no temporary source of water is available, such as a house next door, you will have to have the well dug and temporarily wired for your brick masons who will be needed shortly, or they will have to truck in their own water.

I also recommend, and some locales require, a portable toilet on the job site. Sources for renting these can be found in the Yellow Pages under Toilet-portable.

4. Footings (1 day)

The footing is the base of a structure. It is a mass of concrete supporting the foundation of the house. It can be poured into wooden forms or in trenches. It must be below the *frost line*, or it will heave when the ground thaws and freezes. In the northern states and higher eleva-

tions of any area, it may be four or more feet below grade level. This is one reason there are more basements in a northern climate. If you have to be several feet below the grade for your footing, and thus need several feet of foundation to get back up to grade level, only excavations and a concrete slab are needed for a basement. Local codes will clearly state the requirements for footings in your area. The subcontractor you choose should know the code.

I have a footing sub who stakes, clears, excavates, digs, and pours footings. With a little effort, you can find the same. For your first house, I recommend that you do. The cost will be about the same. The footing is probably the most important part of the house. If it settles or moves, so will your house. If it is not done according to the dimensions of your plans, you will either have to change the plans to accommodate the footing, or do the footing over. I recommend the former if the situation should arise, unless the deviation is too severe to live with.

After your foundation walls are up, you should put in a footing drain. Your code may require this. The drain can be connected to a dry well, storm sewer, or any other approved means of getting rid of the water. In some places, it can simply drain into your yard.

As a rule, footings are better today than they were 100 years ago. Well-built houses of today will probably last more years than those built long ago. Technology has improved materials such as concrete, and our knowledge of how to use them. I say this to help ease your mind about this important step.

Building inspectors usually check the locations of footings before they are poured, to make certain they are deep enough, and resting on undisturbed earth. Don't complain about this inspection — it could save you thousands of dollars if it meant you were avoiding some future problem.

5. Foundations (1 week)

Foundations can be made of brick, concrete block, or poured concrete. Stone foundations, as a rule, aren't built anymore, as they aren't as strong as the others. Stone can be applied as a veneer just like brick, for aesthetic purposes, and you would be wise to use it only as such. Local codes may prohibit stone as a foundation load-bearing material.

Your masonry contractor needs to be one of your better subs. Next to your carpenter, he or she is the most important. Your carpenter probably can recommend a good mason and usually starts work soon after, if not directly after, the mason is finished. If he or she followed a bad one, having to *shim* walls or make an out-of-square foundation work as well as possible will be remembered. Houses **can** have square corners. Most of mine do. (Some don't.)

The foundation wall for any type house needs to be high enough so that water (our old friend) will be diverted away from the house by the final grade of the soil around the house. It must also be high enough so that the wood finish and framing of the house will be at least eight inches above the finish grade and thus protected from soil moisture.

A crawl space should be at least eighteen inches high so that you can crawl beneath the house annually to inspect for such things as termite damage. The crawl space walls should have screened openings for ventilation.

If you are planning on a full basement, your foundation walls should be high enough so that you have at least seven feet four inches of head space in the finished basement.

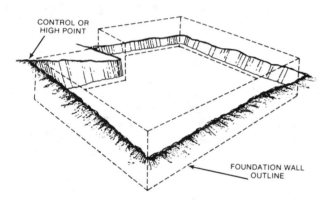

How to establish the depth of excavation.

If you are in doubt about the foundation height, consult an engineer. Usually you, with the help of the carpenter, mason, excavator, or anyone who can use a transit or a level, can determine the needed height. If the lot is almost flat, the job is simple. It becomes tricky when the lot is steep, or has opposing grades. Experienced contractors make certain the foundation is high enough at the highest point of the outline of the foundation wall, and use that highest point as the control point.

The finished foundation should be *waterproofed* from the footing to the finish gradeline. I recommend hiring a professional waterproofing company for this. Companies are listed in the Yellow pages under waterproofing. Don't

let a laborer do it. A professional company will stand behind its work.

Also, depending on your locale, you may need to have the soil treated for insects and pests, particularly termites. Hire a professional. This job is done after the foundation is in, but before any concrete is poured for either the basement or the garage. The cost is small.

It may come as a surprise to many first-time home builders that the foundation is poured or formed with concrete blocks, then holes are punched in it for such things as the water supply and the sewage outlet, the pipe is placed through the hole, and the space between the pipe and wall is patched. This is the easiest method to use to get a tight, waterproof fit.

6. Rough-in Plumbing (2–4 days)

If you have a basement with plumbing or if you are building the house on a concrete slab (as opposed to wood floor joists), once the foundation is in and backfilled and tamped (packed down), and the soil treated, your plumber needs to install the sewer line and the water pipes that will be under the concrete. Also, any wiring that will have to be under the concrete needs to be placed in conduit and roughed-in. Most wiring though, can be run through the stud walls and ceiling joists to any given point.

Your soil treatment company may want to wait until the rough-ins are completed before treating the soil so it won't be disturbed by digging in the plumbing lines. Ask about the policy of the company you choose.

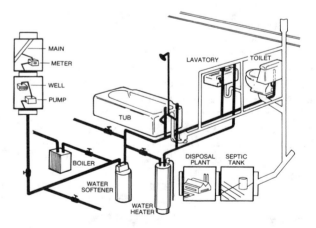

The plumbing system of a home. Note that the supply system pipes are black, the drainage system's are white.

7. Slabs — for Heated Areas (1–2 days)

Many locales require slab perimeter insulation. This is one-inch Styrofoam run around the perimeter four inches high and eighteen inches wide. I recommend it, even if it is not required by codes. I also recommend using a four to six mil thickness vapor barrier of polyurethane (poly) under the concrete to prevent moisture from working up into the concrete. A six by six-inch #10 wire mesh should be placed in the concrete to reinforce it.

The top of the slab should be at least eight inches above the finish grade. Your sub should put down a base for the slab, tamping down gravel or crushed stone to form a layer four to six inches in depth. The poly goes down on this just prior to pouring the concrete. If you cannot cover the entire area with one sheet of poly, any joints of the poly should overlap by four inches and be sealed. The wire mesh is laid on top of the poly. Call for an inspection before pouring concrete if your code requires it.

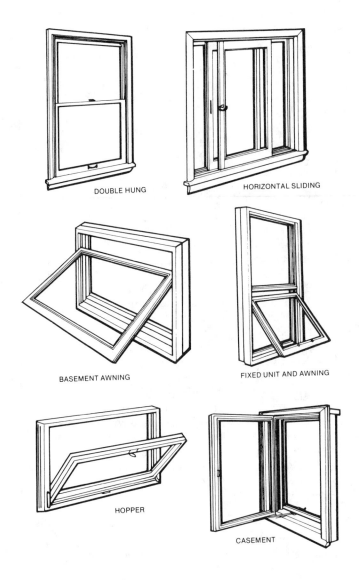

DOUBLE HUNG · HORIZONTAL SLIDING

BASEMENT AWNING · FIXED UNIT AND AWNING

HOPPER · CASEMENT

Various types of windows.

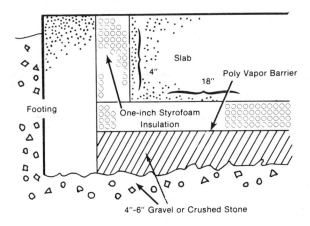

Slab

4″ · 18″ · Poly Vapor Barrier

Footing

One-inch Styrofoam Insulation

4″–6″ Gravel or Crushed Stone

Proper insulation for a concrete slab.

A good concrete sub will do all of this. I stopped checking my slab pourings three years ago when I found a terrific concrete subcontractor.

For garage slabs, with proper backfilling and tamping, you don't need the wire mesh, but if you believe the added strength is needed, use it. I recommend an *expansion joist* of fiber board around the perimeter. Garages are subject to extreme temperature changes, and concrete expands and contracts with those changes. The expansion joint permits this expansion without cracking the concrete. Both this slab and the house slab should be at least four inches thick. Be sure your sub thickens all slabs wherever they will be carrying load-bearing posts or walls. Codes differ on the additional thickness required, but it is often the thickness of the footings.

8. Framing (1–3 weeks)

If you have a good carpenter, this is the end of this section on framing. And if that sounds too simple, wait and see. You need only order the lumber, the windows, and the exterior doors, and in two or three weeks you'll have a house (or at least something that looks like a house). I have included here a typical order list for framing and drying-in, which means making the house secure from rain. Rain or snow during framing is not desirable, but it seldom does much damage beyond an occasional warped piece of lumber. But once the house is dried-in, the work inside can progress regardless of the weather if windows and doors are in place.

Framing List

15 pieces	2 x 6 x 12 treated pine
10 pieces	2 x 4 x 12 treated pine
20 lineal feet	2 x 2
250 lineal feet	1 x 4
18 pieces	2 x 8 x 12
80 pieces	2 x 8 x 14
80 pieces	2 x 8 x 16
55 pieces	2 x 10 x 12
100 pieces	2 x 10 x 14
18 pieces	2 x 10 x 16
18 pieces	2 x 10 x 18
2 pieces	2 x 10 x 20
14 pieces	2 x 6 x 14
45 pieces	2 x 6 x 16
80 pieces	2 x 6 x 20
800 pieces	West Coast studs, 2 x 4 x 93
175 pieces	Half-inch CDX plywood
24 quarts	Plywood glue
10 rolls	#15 felt
60 pieces	Asphalt impregnated sheathing ½ x 4 x 8
300 pounds	16d nails, coated
150 pounds	8d nails, coated
10 pounds	Steel cut masonry 8d
25 pounds	⅞-inch galvanized roofing nails
50 pounds	1¼-inch galvanized roofing nails
10 pounds	16d galavanized finish nails
150 pieces	2 x 4 x 14
50 pieces	2 x 4 x 10

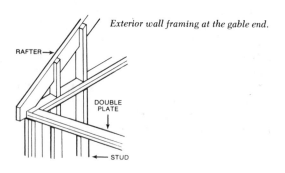

Exterior wall framing at the gable end.

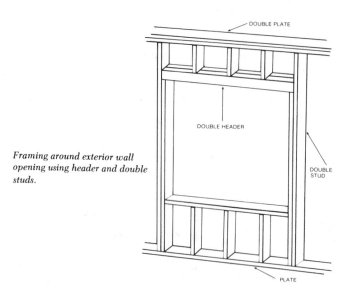

Framing around exterior wall opening using header and double studs.

You will want to check, via phone or in person, with your carpenter about any problems with materials. It is in this stage that I recommend installing a job site telephone. Your carpenter can take it home at night to prevent misuse. If you don't want the expense of a telephone, other arrangements for more frequent communication can be made, such as using a nearby phone, or more frequent visits by you or someone else for you. But since it is impossible to estimate exact needs in materials, some ordering will have to be done. You could give your carpenter permission to order what is needed and then tell the supply house what you have done. The decision is up to you. I do it.

The cross sections of typical framing here are to make you familiar with some of the construction terms.

When the framing is completed, order cabinets, bookcases, and bath vanity cabinets, if there are any. Space for them can now be measured on the job by the salesperson.

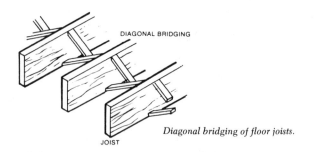

Diagonal bridging of floor joists.

9. Exterior Siding, Trim, Veneer (1–3 weeks)

This phase of construction is carried on while work progresses inside and should be done before roof shingles are installed. Masonry chimneys are installed after siding or veneer. Veneers such as brick should be installed before final exterior trim (boxing) is added. At completion of this step, you are ready for exterior painting.

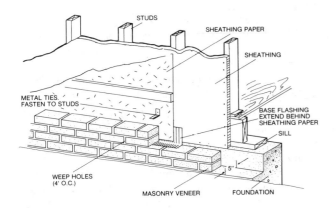

A wood frame wall with masonry veneer. Note shelf on foreground of foundation, to support bricks.

10. Chimneys and Roofing (2 days–1 week)

Chimneys should be built before the roof is shingled. This will allow placement of sheet metal flashing around the chimney for waterproofing, and will also avoid damage to the shingles. A *prefab fireplace* and *flue* would also be installed at this time. Roofing follows completion of the chimneys.

11. Rough-ins (1–2 weeks)

All electrical, plumbing, heating and air-conditioning, phone prewires, stereo and intercom, and burglar alarm systems, should be roughed-in at this time or anytime after step 8 is completed. This does not mean that these units are installed at this time — only the wiring or plumbing for them. Inspections are needed when this step is complete.

12. Insulation (3 days)

Consult with your local utility company on the insulation you need to qualify for their lowest rates. Some locales require an inspection of insulation by both the utility and the building inspection department when it is completed, and before it is covered with drywall or paneling (or plaster, if anyone still wants plaster walls).

13. Hardwood Flooring and Underlayment (3 days–1 week)

I find it easier to install hardwood flooring and carpet or vinyl underlayment before I have the drywall installed. It can be done afterward.

14. Drywall (2 weeks)

Most residential walls are drywalled with ½″ x 4′ x 8′ gypsum wallboard sheets called drywall or Sheetrock. For baths and other moist areas use a waterproof board, or paint it with an enamel paint, even before wallpapering.

Figure on 3½ or 4 times the square footage of floor area for the total square footage of wallboard to be used. Your drywall sub can give you a price based on a square foot charge. Some will give a bid that includes materials. On your first house you may want to go this route.

15. Prime Walls (2 days)

After the drywall is finished and before the interior trim is applied, I prime all walls and ceilings with a flat white latex paint. My two painters do this with a spray gun and can do in one day a house that measures 3,000 square feet. By priming first, the finish painting time is reduced considerably, thus saving you money. With no trim installed, only windows need to be protected during spraying. If all of your woodwork (trim) is going to be painted, instead of being stained, priming the walls by spraying can be postponed until the painting stage.

When the walls and ceilings are primed, the slight imperfections that sometimes occur in finishing drywall will show up. At this time you can have your drywall subcontractor touch up these places so that the walls and ceiling will be ready for final painting (this is called *pointing up*). Pointing up can also be done just after the interior trim is finished in case the walls get nicked during this process. I have done it *both* times, and at no extra charge.

16. Interior Trim (1–2 weeks)

Doors, moldings, cabinets, and shelves are installed at this time. Cabinets that were ordered after the completion of step 8 should be ready for delivery and installation. The cost of installation should be worked out in advance between you and either your carpenter or supplier (or cabinetmaker if you use shop-built cabinets). Interior trim labor usually includes standard trim and moldings. Any special molding or trim work, or paneling, should be discussed with your carpenter in the planning stages to determine the extra cost of installation. Your millwork supplier, usually the lumber company, can do a complete material take-off for your trim and discuss costs of extra items.

17. Painting (2–3 weeks)

You are ready for final painting inside. Your exterior painting can be delayed until this time, too, to save your painter from hopping back and forth from job to job. Work this out when you first discuss painting with your sub. You don't want to leave the exterior trim unpainted or unstained too long, as it may warp or get moldy.

18. Other Trims (1 day–1 week)

It's time to install counter tops, vinyl floors, and ceramic tiles. Wallpaper can be done at this time, or delayed until after you move in. The others can't be delayed, because plumbing cannot be completed until they are.

19. Trim Out (1–2 weeks)

It's time for the plumber to finish work. This is called trimming out or setting fixtures. Some of the fixtures installed must be wired, so he or she needs to finish before the electrician can finish. Also, your heating and air-conditioning must be completed before your electrician finishes work. Next comes your electrician, to install switches, receptacles (sometimes called devices), light fixtures, and electrical appliances, such as the oven and range. He or she will also wire the electrical apparatus that has been installed by your plumber and heating and air-conditioning subs.

20. Clean up (2–3 days)

Both inside and outside cleaning can be started. The bulk of outside trash, and an incredible amount of it comes from inside, can be picked up by truck and hauled away. You can do the inside work. If you don't want to, you can get a professional. Cost depends on the size of the house and the number of windows to be washed, inside and out.

21. Carpet (3 days–1 week)

Hardwood floors should be finished before the carpet is installed. Allow at least three days for hardwood finishing. No other subs should be working in the house while this work is done. They are expensive floors, and it is well worth a few days of "no trespassing" to have them done right. They should be finished before the carpet is installed because of the sanding required before the floors are stained and sealed with polyurethane. The dust from sanding usually is controlled, but some could permeate the rooms with carpeted floors.

Because of this dust, you may want to finish the floors before step 20, cleaning up. I've done it both ways, and found advantages to both.

22. Driveway (1–3 days)

You should keep heavy trucks off newly laid concrete or asphalt drives for a period of time. Try to time it so that you have received all heavy shipments of materials, and hauled off all heavy loads of trash, and don't have any heavy equipment coming to do work. Realize that if you wait until last with the driveway, you'll at least have a moving van on it. Concrete can take a moving van a week after the concrete was poured; not so with asphalt. If you use asphalt, wait until after you move in to pave. Put down a good stone base on the drive before moving in. My asphalt paving contractor insists on this and puts down the stone base and then redoes the stone (or dresses it up) before paving it with asphalt several days after the moving van leaves.

23. Landscaping (1–3 days)

This is an item that, depending on the requirements of your lender, can be put off until after you move in. This situation may arise due to weather or scheduling problems or lack of money due to other cost overruns at the end of construction. You might get by with just grading and seeding, or mulching disturbed wooded areas.

24. Final Inspections, Surveys, Loan Closings (1-3 days)

After the completion of the actual house (not the drive and landscaping, all final inspections from the county or city, for building, electrical, mechanical, and plumbing should be made. Also, the lender will make a final inspection at this time, and may require drives and landscaping to be complete before it will disburse the balance of the construction loan and close it out to the permanent mortgage.

When approval is given, your attorney will coordinate the necessary paperwork and schedule the loan(s) closing. The lender will most likely require a final survey to be sure no additional structures or additions have been placed on the lot in violation of deed restrictions or zoning. Generally, your attorney will order this final survey and any other necessary documents required for closing.

The actual loan closing will only take about fifteen minutes, depending on the efficiency of the attorney and the lender. One document you will want to remember on your own, but you will be reminded of by your attorney or lender, is your insurance policy. It will need to be converted into a homeowners' policy prior to closing. This merely takes a phone call to the agent who issued you your builders' risk (or fire) policy.

25. Enjoy

CHAPTER 9

Additions to an Existing Home

IF YOU ALREADY have a house, but would like more room and don't want to move, you can add to your present home. This option would also require less money than building a bigger house, since you have a house purchased when houses were cheaper to build. An addition may be the solution for you. It could be easier than you think. You may already have a head start toward additional space.

There are two basic ways to add to a home. One is to make habitable an existing unfinished area such as a basement, garage, screened porch, breezeway, or attic. This is the least expensive way because you already have a room, foundation, and some or all of the outside walls. The other and more expensive way is to build on to your house. If you consider this, check to see that you have room on your lot without violating required setbacks and that you meet any subdivision or deed restrictions.

Don't add too much value to your home. You don't want to have the most expensive house in the neighborhood. It's a real estate fact of life: the $100,000 house in the $50,000 neighborhood is very difficult to sell.

Whether you finish an existing space or add to your present structure, the procedure will be the same. Start at the beginning of this book and treat the addition as a small home. The only things that will be different from building a house are that you already have the land and the costs will be somewhat different. Don't skip any of the applicable steps I outlined earlier for building a house. You will need an attorney to check restrictions and for the loan, plans, an estimate, and the money to build. Look at the end of Chapter 5 before deciding to do your own labor.

How to Estimate Costs

The basic differences in estimating an addition against a complete home will be the elimination of some costs due to the existing structure and the increase of some square foot costs due to the smaller size of the job. Subs may want a few more dollars for their labor costs because they could be earning more for almost the same amount of time.

The general contractor that you won't need would have charged a greater percentage for profit and overhead for the same reason as the subs. This savings will more than offset the increase in labor costs from subs.

You should obtain bids (quotes), as though you were building a house, and proceed from there.

How to Finance an Addition

Financing an addition is far easier than financing a new home. You can simply get a *second mortgage* based on the equity you have in your home. Your equity is the difference between what the house is worth and what you owe on it. Quite often you don't even need to give a reason to borrow against that equity because the lender is well protected if you should default. The house exists, it is not being built. The amount you can borrow varies from lender to lender but if you have been in your house for at least three years it is safe to assume you have built up some equity. As a rule of thumb you can borrow up to one-half of your equity. The second mortgage, which is usually a five- to ten-year loan, is less expensive per month and in total pay–back than refinancing the whole house or building a new house of equal dollar value at high mortgage rates.

Just as in planning new home construction, your local lender can sit down with you and discuss your needs.

Part II

MANAGE YOUR OWN HOME RENOVATION

CHAPTER 10

Finding a Restorable Structure

REHABILITATION, RESTORATION, REMODELING, and renovation are words that mean very close to the same thing. Rehabilitation means to bring back, as does restoration. Remodel and renovate indicate changing something. I am going to use all four words interchangeably at times, so if you are a purist, please forgive me. The word I'll be using the most, however, is restoration. I call an old structure that can be recycled or made habitable an R.O.S., a restorable old structure.

Restorable Old Structures

First, what is an old structure (O.S.)? For the purpose of this book, it shall be any building whatsoever which, due to old age, neglect, or having been used for purposes other than habitation, is not suitable for habitation today. Or, if it is habitable, it is barely or not preferably so. This means that our O.S. can be an inner-city, country, or even a suburban structure. Inner-city O.S.'s can be brownstones, row houses, old stores, apartments over stores, lofts, even factories, and bungalows. A country O.S. can be a barn, an old farmhouse, a carriage house, an old mill or anything else one happens to find when scouring the countryside — even a church. A suburban building can and most likely will be an older house, although there are many forms of old commercial structures in the suburbs.

I define an R.O.S. as an O.S. that can be restored (rehabilitated, remodeled, or renovated) at a reasonable cost. Cost will be the primary determining factor as to whether or not an O.S. is, in fact, an R.O.S. It is not the only factor, for location, aesthetics, and personal needs and tastes are important, too. Obviously, if you have an unlimited budget, or for reasons of proximity or aesthetics want to restore an O.S. even if the costs become unfeasible, you should use other determining factors that I will discuss shortly.

Except in rare cases, the cost of the process of restoration, rehabilitation, or remodeling plus the cost of the O.S. should not exceed the cost of a comparable new structure. Therefore, an R.O.S. is an O.S. that can be restored at a cost that makes restoration feasible.

You may be surprised to discover what is restorable. A house totally burned to the ground can be restored less expensively than a new one can be built. That's an extreme example, of course, but the reasoning applies to O.S.'s in better condition. Obviously, if you start with something, you will have more than if you started with nothing. In the case of the burned-out house, you would be starting with a foundation, concrete slabs, driveways, and a cleared lot. If you have to pay full market value (new value) for this O.S. in such a state, it would behoove you to go elsewhere. But if you could purchase it quite cheaply, as you would most likely be able to, you'd be ahead of the game.

Finding an O.S. for which cosmetic improvement will suffice is more difficult than finding an R.O.S. in need of more costly repair. But, they exist and can be found. Obviously, these O.S.'s are, or were, dwelling units to begin with, as opposed to nonresidential O.S.'s that require conversion. Some good examples of structures suitable for cosmetic improvement can be found among farmhouses, row houses and brownstones, or one-family houses, especially in old neighborhoods.

Why Buy an Old Structure?

The obvious reason is, of course, to save money. An R.O.S. presumably will cost less than a comparable new structure, especially if you are your own general contractor. There are other reasons for buying an O.S. that are quite valid, but these will vary in importance with each individual. Just as some people are fond of antiques and find in them great warmth, beauty, or quality, many see a beauty in O.S.'s that others don't. Their prime concern in restoring an O.S. is aesthetics; cost considerations are secondary. Some may be interested in an O.S. because of its proximity to their work, shopping, or friends. In most urban areas if proximity to the heart of the city is desired, an O.S. is one of few alternatives. Others may want just the opposite — the country is for them. Preservation of the past is a motivating concern to some. They will restore an O.S. to save it from demolition. Many feel that the housing developments built in the past thirty years leave much to be desired, lacking individuality, warmth, and charm.

You can make a remodeling, rehabilitation, restoration, or renovation project as difficult or easy as you want. The main disadvantage in doing a project, as opposed to buying a new property — if indeed it can be called a disadvantage — is, if *you* permit the project to become too complicated, it can overwhelm you. I will show you the simple approach and encourage you to maintain the right frame of mind. You must bend and compromise when necessary and not become discouraged.

Use Your Imagination

Some people can look at something that is unfinished and envision precisely how it is going to look when finished. An artist, for example, knows this when the painting is just begun. I, as a builder, know precisely what a house is going to look like before I ever begin. In my mind's eye, I picture it sitting on a particular lot. I also can see a shabby wreck of a structure and picture it totally restored, even to the colors, all in my mind. I feel all of us have this ability to some extent. It is enhanced by experience, but all experience does is give us the confidence to use what was there all along — our imagination. If you allow yourself to try, you will be able to look at an R.O.S. and imagine what it will look like restored, even if you have never tried before. You must do so or you won't even be motivated to attempt the renovation and you won't have that thrill of seeing your goal, the finished renovation, in front of you.

It isn't necessary to visualize how the interior will look, and quite honestly, some of them will look so bad you may not be able to envision a new interior. The inside design will be visualized and drawn out in plans by your architect or designer. Of course, some R.O.S.'s will be in good enough shape that no imagination will be necessary. Just don't get turned off by all of the filth and trash that you may find inside an R.O.S. or by holes in walls and floors, missing windows, ripped out plumbing and wiring, and so on. That is all relatively minor as you will soon realize. The best way to look at the inside of an R.O.S. is with your eyes partially closed, with just a fuzz of light filtering through your eyelids, and *then* use your imagination. If it is really bad, close your eyes completely!

Making an Informed Search

Obviously, the final decision to buy and restore an R.O.S. is yours, but it helps to have preliminary information when you are searching, or deciding whether or not a given structure in a particular area is a wise choice, or if money is going to be available to you, or if you can afford to do it. Advice on these matters is absolutely free and should be sought out and added to your knowledge of your own situation.

Real estate brokers can give you good input regarding a structure in a particular area. Be sure that their input isn't tempered with self-interest.

Savings and loans can give you the same information as real estate brokers and it may be less biased. They can also discuss your money needs and their loan qualification procedures. A visit to a savings and loan office would be one of my first steps in deciding to restore an R.O.S. Find a lender you feel comfortable with. Savings and loans are not all created equal and certainly not staffed equally. If you feel uncomfortable with one, try another. You'll have a rapport with one sooner or later. Don't be intimidated. Their business is to lend you money; that's how they make money.

Prioritizing Your Search: Location, Cost, Design

Priorities need to be established in order to find an R.O.S. that is suitable for you. You will establish these priorities, but they will be based on where you want to live (location), how much you can and want to spend (cost), and what type of R.O.S. suits you (design).

Where to look is going to be based on whether you want to live in, near, or far away from the city. This then is the starting point and the first priority — location. Decide this point first and let the other two priorities, cost and design, follow in that order. There will, of course, be exceptions. You can also have an R.O.S. moved. House moving is expensive, but it is done every day. Professional house movers are listed in the Yellow Pages.

Cost, of course, will be determined by what you can afford to spend. I will give you all the guidelines; the rest is up to you. You must let your budget be your guide in the end — unless you have an unlimited budget. However, I have found that even extremely wealthy people have a budget and adhere to it.

Skipping ahead to design, I would no more recommend a particiular style or period than I would recommend what color shirt you should wear. I will make recommendations regarding interior space design, as this is often a matter of practicality rather than personal preference.

When your three priorities are established at least tentatively, you could then do what I would do — turn the search process over to one of my key individuals, the real estate broker. I would tell the broker what my priorities are and request that the search be confined by the constraints that those priorities impose.

What to Look For in Buying a Restorable Old Structure

There are several items that are important when looking for an R.O.S. First, the structure. The actual in-depth examination of an R.O.S. needs to be done by a pro, another of your key individuals, the inspection engineer. But there are a few very simple things that you can look for that will allow you to make a quick go/no-go decision:

- the neighborhood — What is it like?
- zoning — What will the neighborhood look like in the future?
- fire insurance rates — Are they high, low, astronomical?
- property taxes — Will they rise rapidly or remain steady?
- security — Is there loitering in neighborhood, windows barred?

The neighborhood can be very important so while you are examining your prospective R.O.S., take a look around. Would you like to live here? Better yet, would you, or could you, if you had to? Maybe it is in the midst of rehabilitation and you love it. At any rate, look — it is important. What's over there a block away — a trash dump? Who are your neighbors going to be, now and in the future? Will you like them? Will you fear them?

Some of your questions won't have an answer, at least not an immediate answer. You will need to talk to others. If there are people there who have already renovated an R.O.S., talk to them. They won't mind. In fact, they will be glad to see more potential rehabilitation coming into the neighborhood. It enhances their property value. Of course, that could prejudice their advice to you. Talk to lenders who may be pushing for rehabilitation in the area, talk to your real estate broker if you used one. If not, call a real estate agency that handles sales in the area. Most real estate brokers will be honest with you; their reputation is at stake.

In the country, you can usually be less concerned about the neighborhood, but you still need to look around. Is that a pig farm down the road? Very odorous, indeed!

Zoning is supposed to mean that what you see around the neighborhood today, you will also see tomorrow. That's a rather flippant definition of a serious topic, but it is true. Zoning is important and yet some cities and locales don't have it. You (or your real estate broker — another reason to have one) will need to check to see if your locale has zoning and if it does, what it does for you. Zoning is supposed to keep residential neighborhoods residential, business neighborhoods business, and industrial neighborhoods industrial. But often there is spot zoning allowed which mixes business with residential. Sometimes that is good, often it is bad. In the country, zoning is just as important. Do you want a gas station built next to your restored farmhouse?

Sometimes other things, such as *deed restrictions*, do the same as zoning and these can protect you, but not for as wide a geographical area as zoning can. Your attorney and/or your real estate broker can advise you about zoning and deed restrictions. It is their field of expertise. That's what they are there for — use them!

Fire insurance is an item I hesitate to mention, for it is a rather negative one, but in good conscience I can't leave it out. Some areas are considered a worse fire risk than others, and this can seriously affect the amount of money one pays for fire insurance. The rate that one pays is partially determined by how long it takes the fire department to respond and the probability of fire in a particular neighborhood. Obviously, if you live twenty miles from the nearest volunteer fire department, the chances are slim your home could be saved in the event of fire (although most likely *you* would be saved by a smoke detector). The insurance company would then have a large claim to pay. Therefore, you will pay higher rates. The same would be true if you lived in a neighborhood with a high rate of arson. Many factors affect rates, and you will need to make a quick call to your insurance agent to see if there is a problem. Most likely there won't be, but better safe than sorry.

Property taxes are usually based on the property's value, so these taxes can be, and often are, escalated drastically as a neighborhood and/or a dwelling is improved. Some locales, in order to encourage rehabilitation, promise little or no increase in taxes. Some couldn't care less and tax away at the new value you have given (or will give) your R.O.S. Be sure to call your county tax agent, or have your real estate broker find out what your taxes will be now and what they will be when your project is finished. They could increase by over $1,000 per year, so be careful.

Security can be a problem. But this is the last discouraging part, so cheer up! Some R.O.S.'s will be found in isolated areas, in or adjacent to run-down neighborhoods, or near commercial areas. This often, but not always, presents a security problem.

In the case of inner-city rehabilitation (urban renewal),

there is often less crime as neighbors are more watchful due to a more acute awareness of potential crime. Most crime in this country consists of daytime robberies and no area — new or old, rich or poor — is immune. If I were concerned about a particular area I would talk to the police, neighbors, real estate brokers, and savings and loans which lend in that area. I also recommend considering the installation of a burglar alarm. There are many models to choose from, and they range from simple to sophisticated. Their costs range accordingly. You can do the installation yourself with components from an electronics store, or you can call a security alarm company listed in the Yellow Pages.

If the O.S. is suitable to you by these criteria you or your real estate broker need only quickly look for the obvious defects that could prove costly. Until your inspection engineer does a thorough exam, you won't be able to determine actual restoration costs. But to keep you from needing to call the engineer more than once or twice, first look for these obvious defects:

- serious fire damage
- severe sagging of the roof
- severe leaning of a wall or walls
- crumbling or wide cracks in the foundation.

What is severe? How wide is wide? There is, unfortunately, no concrete answer (pardon the pun!). Let common sense prevail and remember, it is going to be examined by a pro. Your main concern will be to select an O.S. that is in a place you are willing to live and in good enough condition that your construction engineer won't think you are *non compos mentis* when he sees it.

Buy the Worst in the Best Neighborhood

It is probably more judicious to say "buy the cheapest in the best neighborhood." That way you allow for the fact that the worst isn't always the cheapest and vice versa.

Why would you want the cheapest? It is a real estate fact of life that the lowest priced house in a neighborhood *appreciates* the fastest and is more assured of appreciation in the first place. One should always think of the resale value of a home, and if you own the most expensive home in the neighborhood it is usually the hardest to sell. This happens for two reasons: (1) as the price gets higher, the market, or number of *qualified buyers*, gets smaller; (2) many people are aware of the fact that you shouldn't buy the most expensive house in the neighborhood. More and more people are realizing that they don't need large homes — at least not as large as they once would have considered. High energy costs and changing lifestyles that leave less time to care for a large home have precipitated this thinking. So stay toward the low- to middle-price range if possible. This also means that you will probably be purchasing a smaller R.O.S. making your restoration costs lower. As you will see, there is a direct proportion of size to cost.

CHAPTER 11

Is the Structure Restorable?

Architect/Designer

An architect/designer is more important in restoration than in new construction. The reason is that in new construction there are thousands of ready made *building plans* and *specifications* available. In custom designing, of course, the need for an architect/designer is obvious, and in restoring an O.S., there are a few particulars that warrant an architect/designer. Of course, if you are only going to paint and move in, you would not need an architect/designer. But once you decide to undertake major remodeling, restoration, or rehabilitation, you need a plan. This plan can be very simple or very elaborate. It will always consist of a master plan showing what is going to be done to the structure item by item, room by room. The master plan includes *blueprints* that show what the dimensions of each finished room will look like, and specifications that describe the materials to be used. Based on cost considerations, the master plan will determine what the blueprints and specifications will be. Theoretically, you could do the master plan yourself, but without spending too much money you can also get some expert advice from an architect/designer. The expertise and experience of an architect/designer can save you more money than it will cost, as the two of you determine together what to do to your R.O.S. You will both go through each room and decide what, if anything other than cosmetic improvements, to do to it. If walls are to be moved or eliminated, you will need the architect/designer's advice as to which can be moved without adding structural support. If additional structural support is necessary, either as a result of changes or because of an existing bad condition, he is the person who will design such supports. Other structural defects can be remedied on the architect/designer's advice, based on both the inspection engineer's report and his or her own evalua-

tion. He or she will obviously have to physically inspect the R.O.S., too. You'll decide, based on this opinion, whether you can live with prevailing structural, plumbing, electrical, or energy conditions, or if you should change them. This advice will guide you concerning the inclusion of such new technologies and modernizations as solar adaptations, saunas, and hot tubs.

The exterior of your R.O.S. will need careful evaluation for proper restoration based on aesthetics, structural preservation, and cost. Here again, an architect or designer's advice can be time- and money-saving. Perhaps you thought you had to do more than you really needed. Perhaps you will be advised not to spend $10,000 for new siding; all you need is a few rotten boards replaced, a sanding or sandblasting, and a paint job — for about half what you planned to spend. An extreme example, but viable, nonetheless.

Aesthetics are a very important consideration in an R.O.S. There needs to be expert guidance in determining what the finished product will look like. Without it you could end up spending a lot of money unnecessarily and have a terrible looking restored R.O.S. — called "re-muddling." I have seen them and my first thought is "what a waste of time and money." This is not to say that you have no input about what your R.O.S. will look like. You will determine that. You simply need expert advice. You could gain limited expertise from reading books and journals on old house restoration, and it wouldn't hurt to do so, even if you employ an architect/designer. But there is no substitute for the give-and-take in a conversation with an expert who can answer your questions and help you make decisions. Such invaluable suggestions as adding a dormer to make use of an attic can come from your architect/designer, and give you inexpensive additional space.

Architects generally work for a fee based on a percentage of the project's cost or by the hour. With a percentage of cost, you run the risk of having the cost deliberately run higher than it need be. The percentage charged will vary depending on whether you want the architect to supervise construction or not. Obviously, it is going to cost you money for full supervision, and you don't really need it. Architects generally provide this service as a liaison between owner and general contractor. Since you are both, you don't need a liaison. You could still have the architect supervise if you feel inadequate or have him or her supervise on a part-time, as-needed basis. Otherwise, the architect's job will be finished prior to construction and will consist of only design, consulation, and blueprints and specifications. For this the fee would be a percentage of project cost.

A home designer is less expensive but not necessarily less knowledgeable than an architect. He or she may work on the same fees/services plans described above, but designers will often work for a fee based on the square footage of the R.O.S. and will also supervise when needed on an hourly or percentage-of-cost basis, usually at a lower cost than an architect.

Again, proper advice and planning is extremely important and will save you money in the long run. Proper advice and planning can also show you ways to postpone certain items in order to save money initially. I'll discuss this in more depth later in this chapter.

Inspection Engineer

Prior to finalizing any arrangements with the architect/designer you will need the services of your inspection engineer. The inspection engineer will provide the information that will enable you to decide whether or not to purchase your R.O.S. Conceivably, he or she and your architect/designer could inspect the R.O.S. together, but that is unlikely and an unnecessary expense. An inspection engineer or firm will, for a fee, inspect the following items and, most importantly, guarantee in writing the condition of each. Some inspections are even backed by an insurance policy and I would gravitate toward those who have such insurance. An inspection engineer should also be able to give you an approximate cost of repair for each item, although not an exact cost. This approximate cost will give you a quick estimate that will tell you if you can afford the project. Most inspection engineers do not do repair work for the obvious reason that they would be inviting conflict of interest. Those who sometimes do will spell out explicitly beforehand that the inspection engineer will not be given any of the repair work on this project. You will get a more impartial and objective inspection that way. You will employ this person only when *you* have found an O.S. you believe to be restorable. You may go through this process more than once, I'm sorry to say, but it is better to spend the money in the beginning than to get caught with a very expensive surprise later.

The items the inspection engineer will check and report on are:

1. Foundation — for cracks, settling, water problems, crumbling, heaving;
2. First floor framing *sill* and *plates* and joists — for rotting, insect damage (termites), cracks, settling;
3. Exterior walls, siding, doors and windows, *soffit* and *fascia boards* — for rotting, cracks in veneers such as brick and stone;
4. Roof — for sags, rotting members, life expectancy of shingles;
5. Insulation (a relatively new inspection — to see what insulation there is if any, advise as to needs;
6. Fireplace and chimneys;
7. Water drainage on lot — especially if water damage has been found in basement or *crawl space*;
8. Plumbing — for water pressure, life expectancy of plumbing pipes, condition of fixtures (lavatory, closets, tubs, showers);
9. Electrical — for type and condition of wiring, adequacy of service (power) to structure for current and future needs, condition and safety of electrical devices (receptacles and switches) and fixtures, all *panels* and their *fuses* and *circuit breakers*;
10. Mechanical — for condition and adequacy of any and all heating and air conditioning equipment and its life expectancy;
11. Appliances — (stoves, etc.) for condition of any and all;
12. Well and septic tank, if applicable — for recovery of well (water pressure over long flow period), visible problems with septic tank (standing water in leach or drain field, noticeable odors).

The foundation inspection can be separated from the rest and referred to as a structural inspection. Often that is available by itself at a lower cost, if that is all you need. I recommend the entire inspection if you are going to buy. If you aren't sure due to extremely poor condition of the O.S., then opt for the structural portion of the inspection only. If it passes, or passes for your purposes, then you can proceed with the rest of the inspection. If at all possible, accompany the engineer during the inspection. You can benefit by getting to know the O.S. better, and you'll pick up bits and pieces of information to help you if this one fails to pass muster and you have to continue searching. Don't worry if you can't accompany the inspector.

Advice From Key People

All your key people can offer advice and have specific areas of expertise that enable them to answer any questions that might arise in your decision-making process. By the time you have reached the point of determining if an O.S. is restorable, you should have lined up all of your key people and have talked to them about your project, even about this particular R.O.S. A lender, such as a savings and loan officer, can offer advice based on experience. This advice can pertain to the worth of the neighborhood, how much you should spend, how much value added is too much, and so on. The only one you may not have lined up is the carpenter, but if you have, his or her advice can be beneficial, giving you a more accurate idea of cost pertaining to major woodworking structural changes or repair. The carpenter's time with you in consulting may or may not be free. That will depend on the individual and the scope of the prospective job.

All advice should be treated as such. It is an opinion as to what should be done. Some advice may be bad. The final decision on what will be done is yours and yours alone, but the more expert opinions you have on any matter the easier your decision-making will be.

Advice and opinions should not be confused with necessary technical decisions that must be made initially. No matter how many books you read on the subject or no matter how many expert friends you have, leave technical decisions to the professionals. A decision regarding the structural integrity of an O.S. and what needs to be done to rectify any problems is a decision that can be made only by a professional.

Partial Renovation

There is no "law of restoration" that says an O.S. has to be totally redone. It is often economically beneficial to do only those things that will make the structure habitable. This definition will vary for each individual as some can live without things that others can't and some can live with some things that others can't. Some things can be fixed later — years later. You can do one room at a time, or parts of a room at a time. One important criteria must be met however; the structure must be safe in all ways — structurally, electrically, and so on. Some locales have habitation standards for dwellings, but some don't. We are considering so many O.S.'s, however, that the possible degrees of habitation are quite numerous. There is no set answer to what you should, shouldn't, could, or couldn't do in lieu of total rehabilitation or restoration. What is important to you will prevail, governed by your budget and common sense (and your inspection engineer's report). The need for a master plan is as great, if not greater, under these circumstances.

My personal preferences as to comfort would lead me to do as much to the kitchen and bath(s) as I could afford. Cleaning, painting, and other cosmetics would then suffice. If the electrical wiring needed replacing, it can be done without removing the plaster walls. In fact, you probably can get by without replacing all the wiring. Plumbing can be replaced without too much wall repair. Maybe the pipes will last another two years or so. The general idea is to do what is necessary *now* and put off other renovation. Of course, if you are starting with a barn ...

Another point to keep in mind when considering partial remodeling is the total value of the end product. I have stated before that you don't want to make the house too valuable for the neighborhood. Partial restoration is a way to control your total cost and keep it from adding too much value too quickly.

What do you do when you find that your O.S. is an R.O.S., but it is going to cost too much or you feel it will be too expensive for the neighborhood. Well, if partial renovation can't or won't fit your particular situation, you will have to continue your search for an R.O.S. You must remain logical and unemotional (don't fall in love with an O.S.) in your decision-making process.

CHAPTER 12

Is the Renovation Feasible?

BASED ON YOUR inspection report, advice from your other professionals, and your own common sense, judgment, and budget, you can determine which costs will be immediate, which can be eliminated, and which put off until later. In order to do this you need a priority list, a budget, building plans, determination of space requirements, a master plan, plans for additions, a completion timetable, and living arrangements during the project. Let us cover each of these components of feasibility.

Priority List

This is a method I use to place priorities on items pertaining to the project. I try to be objective, but personal preference will influence the list also. Beginning with the inspection engineer's report, I list all the items covered and the report concerning each. If the foundation is basically sound, but there is some settling causing floors to sag above, I need to determine if I want to fix this now or later. It can be done at either time. But if the foundation is crumbling and will probably fall or cave in soon, I would put that repair at the head of my priority list. This list is used to determine whether or not you go ahead with any costs, not just those pertaining to the structure. Use it to determine if you want an architect or designer, central air conditioning or window units, to purchase a new furnace or patch the old, to put in a driveway or not,

to add more landscaping, and so forth. Clearly, that professional inspection engineer's report is crucial.

Priority List

	Top Priority (must spend)	Low Priority (optional)	Don't Need (Ok as is)
1. Inspection fees	√		
2. Design assistance		√	
3. Loan closing costs	√		
4. Construction or short-term loan interest	√		
5. Fire insurance	√		
6. Temporary utilities	√		
7. Cleaning the R.O.S.		√	
8. Plans and specifications	√		
9. Permits and fees	√		
10. Clearing, grading, and excavation for additions			√
11. Footings			√
12. Foundations			√
13. Waterproofing			√

	Top Priority (must spend)	Low Priority (optional)	Don't Need (Ok as is)
14. Tearing out a. exterior walls			√
b. interior walls	√		
c. roof shingles	√		
d. roof rafters			√
e. plaster, drywall			√ (some patching)
f. furnace, radiators	√		
g. plumbing	√		
h. electrical wiring	√		
i. total gutting			√
15. New framing — lumber, materials, and labor a. walls	(2 walls) √		
b. floors			√
c. ceilings			√
d. roof			√
e. additions		√	
16. Steel			√
17. Windows	√		
18. Exterior doors			√ (refinish)
19. Roofing — labor and materials	√		
20. Concrete flatwork			√
21. Exterior trim — labor and materials	√ (facia)		
22. Exterior siding or veneers			√
23. Plumbing — upfitting, per fixture	√		
24. Plumbing — new, per room	√		
25. Heating and A/C	√		
26. Electrical — upfitting	√		
27. Electrical — new wiring and service	√		
28. Insulation — walls, ceilings, and floors	√		
29. Drywall	√ (patching)		
30. Plaster	√ (patching)		
31. Water and sewer main repair			√

	Top Priority (must spend)	Low Priority (optional)	Don't Need (Ok as is)
32. Well and septic system			√
33. Cabinets, bath vanities	√		
34. Interior trim materials			√
35. Interior doors			√
36. Interior trim labor			√
37. Painting, interior	√		
38. Painting, exterior	√		
39. Appliances (built in)	√		
40. Light fixtures		√	
41. Floor coverings	√		
42. Drives, walks, patios			√
43. Cleaning		√	
44. Gutters, screens, miscellaneous	√		
45. Wallpaper		√	
46. Hardware & bath accessories		√	
47. Landscaping			√
48. Miscellaneous allowance			

Special Notes:

I mentioned that such problems as a sagging floor can be corrected later. That's true as long as the sag isn't too great. The inspection engineer should indicate this in a report. If it is too great, it will put unusual vertical and horizontal stress on the *framing* of the structure. Correction is not expensive.

What else can be lived with in order to put off the cost of repair or renovation until later? Other than what your inspection engineer says is important pertaining to the structure, you can live with just about anything that you are willing to put up with! Keep in mind when deciding what to save to do later that it will then cost you a little more to do. This will be due to inflation and the fact that small jobs cost comparatively more than big jobs. You will save overall by getting as much done at once as you can. Also keep in mind the inconvenience you may suffer from having your life disrupted by remodeling after you move in.

Ideally, if your budget permits, I recommend getting all the major jobs done now and pick and sort through the minor ones to see what to put off. The major jobs would be any that involve tearing the old out and replacing with new. This includes plumbing, electrical wiring, mechanical work, foundation, roof, chimneys, plaster, rotten framing, siding, porches, and any appliances that are either just about at the end of their life expectancies or aren't there at all. You don't have to completely remodel a kitchen in order to make it more convenient. A new stove or dishwasher and a coat of paint will do wonders.

If you have an R.O.S. that has nothing as far as kitchen or baths you'll have less to eliminate from your list. But you could eliminate decorative items such as wallpaper, light fixtures, and landscaping.

If your inspection engineer says that the roofing is good for another two to five years, then wait if need be. It may not look so good, but so what?

Budget

All the decisions on your priority list are predicated mainly by the budget that you must prepare *before you even start looking for* an R.O.S. The total cost of the R.O.S. when finished shouldn't exceed what you have predetermined you can afford. You should be cautious in this stage, for it is easy to forget that the total or finished cost of the R.O.S. you are looking at can be considerably higher than what it is selling for now. You can't purchase an R.O.S. unobjectively and then find out once you have purchased it that the renovation will exceed your budget. This sometimes happens, but it won't if you calculate properly. If you determine how much you can afford to borrow and you know how much cash you have to can come up with, you basically know your budget.

Suppose your income warrants a first mortgage of $60,000 and you have $10,000 cash, then set your budget at $70,000 — unless you receive aid through special financing. So if you find an R.O.S. for $20,000 and it is going to cost $50,000 to restore (all costs, from architect to landscaper), you are within your budget. But if the R.O.S. is selling for $40,000 and it is going to cost $55,000 to restore, one of the two amounts is going to have to give, or you are going to have to get some special financing, or you are going to have to look elsewhere for

an R.O.S. Your priority list can help reduce the $50,000 renovation cost. Let your budget be your guide and you'll be protected in your decision.

Sample Budget

Purchase price of R.O.S.		$29,000
Estimated cost of renovation		+$35,000
Total Cost		$64,000
Market (appraised) value when complete		$80,000
Construction loan and permanent financing available when complete (80% of $80,000)	$64,000	
Personal cash invested when complete	+ -0-	
Total Investment		—$64,000
Personal equity when complete		$16,000

Interim Cash Required

Down payment on purchase price (10% — balance by seller, commercial lender, relative)	$ 2,900
Cash needed for interest, pre-construction draw expenses	+$ 5,000
Total personal cash needed during construction	$ 7,900

Note: The permanent loan amount ($64,000) will cover all expenses, including the total purchase price, construction costs, and out-of-pocket expenses ($7,900).

Building Plans

Floor plans or blueprints can be obtained from either an existing set, one that the present owner may have or a set on file with local building departments or historic societies, or they can be drawn for you by an architect or designer (the latter is the most likely case). You can probably sketch out the room sizes on a piece of graph paper, if it is just for your feasibility study. I recommend this method, as it doesn't cost you anything. Simply draw the inside dimensions of each room on a piece of graph paper allowing one foot for each square on the paper. You don't have to draw or sketch the whole R.O.S. as it would appear on a blueprint with each room contiguous. Just be sure to label each room as to its position and use.

Generally, you won't want or need to go through the expense of actual blueprints until you have committed yourself to the purchase of a particular R.O.S. You will need blueprints before you can proceed with actual cost estimating. They should show the structure as is, the way a sketch or floor plan would, and also how it will be when completed, showing any and all changes, additions, and deletions to the structure you plan. The blueprints will or should include a foundation plan, if applicable, floor plans for all floors, and outside *elevations*. Optional features can be a typical wall section, electrical plan, and a mechanical plan for heating and air conditioning.

If you have never looked at a set of blueprints in your life, don't worry. There is no mystery to them. The main function of residential blueprints is to show the floor plan and the design (elevation). They are virtually self-explanatory, but you can go over them with whoever drew the plans to be sure you do understand them. There is no cost for this. Be sure you understand even the items you feel foolish asking about. Your subs will understand the plans and most will use them for price quotes. A sample set of blueprints is included in the Appendix. But remember your designer or architect will go over your blueprints and floor plan as many times as necessary for you to understand them.

Determining Space Requirements

Space requirements are different for different people, and what is adequate for one will be totally inadequate for another. This somewhat obvious statement has a hidden consequence, however, when you employ others to design and draw floor plans for your R.O.S. What is adequate space to them may be inadequate to you. This means living in discomfort although you may save on your renovation costs (smaller usually means less). The opposite is equally bad. You may end up with larger spaces than you need, and spend more than you need on renovation and maintenance as a result. Once again, your budget will have to temper your final decision. But how do you determine what is and what isn't adequate space for you? I find the most foolproof method is to take the floor plan and room by room find another room of equivalent size that already exists. There is no substitute for reality, and I strongly recommend this method. If the kitchen is 12 x 12, find a 12 x 12 kitchen in a friend's house or apartment; or at least find a room that is 12 x 12 and allow for cabinets and appliances. If you have massive furniture, allow for that in other rooms. I also recommend that you "block in" large furniture that will occupy rooms. To do this, cut pieces of graph paper or plain paper to scale and place the pieces on your floor plan. To scale means that if ¼ inch equals 1 foot on your floor plan, then cut the piece of paper to show ¼ inch of paper for each 1 foot of furniture. It doesn't have to be exact, so don't fret over this little chore.

Master Plan

I have referred before to what I call a master plan. Actually, once you prepare your budget, your cost list, your estimate sheet, and your priority list, you pretty well have a master plan. You know what you are and what you are not going to do. But some of the things you have eliminated need to be planned for in the future, and all the items, even though they are on the cost list, need to be written down in a general synopsis so that you can proceed in an orderly fashion. I find the easiest way to do this is to have a drawing, a sketch, or a set of blueprints for the R.O.S. in front of me. Then I can go through each room and make a list of what I am going to do to that room. I do the same thing for the exterior using the elevation. The master plan is refined as you proceed with the other planning stages, since you obviously can't decide what not to do until you find out what it costs and what the entire project costs.

Planning for Additions

If you find that you need more space than the R.O.S. allows, but everything else is what you're looking for, you can consider an addition to the structure. This is usually not difficult and may not be too expensive.

To get more space in one room in the R.O.S., you may want to combine rooms by removing a common wall or cutting a doorway, and then add the room you eliminated back on by building an addition. Additions can, and often do, use existing space within the R.O.S. that was previously not going to be used as living space — for example, attics, basements, storage space, and garages or carports. Utilizing these spaces is usually the least expensive way to add on as you can take advantage of such existing structural components as roofs, walls, and foundations.

Even adding a deck or porch increases, or gives the effect of increasing, living space, as well as adding value to the R.O.S. Discuss this possibility with your architect or designer.

Fireplaces can be added to virtually any room in the structure, especially with today's prefab units. These prefab units are very safe, economical to install, and work well. They are also aesthetically pleasing and in many cases you can't tell the difference between a solid masonry fireplace and a prefab. They are also available in heat recirculating models for saving energy.

How Long It Will Take

The major factor in determining how long any restoration will take is the scope of the job. Obviously, if you are going to *gut* a brownstone or convert a barn, it is going to take longer than a kitchen and bath remodeling job. To determine how long your project will take, add up the time designated for each item in Chapter 14. Use only the items that will apply to your project. (Your architect/designer can help you with this. You may or may not be charged for the time involved — *ask first.* It certainly shouldn't take more than one hour.) Use maximum times to be on the safe side, for it will often take that long and sometimes longer. But don't worry about that now; we will cover that in Chapter 14 and the extra time is usually not important. Other factors that will affect the time it takes to complete the project are weather, availability of labor and materials, municipal inspections, and your own availability to schedule the steps, complete one, and move on to the next. As you will see, minor renovations should take about a month or so and major restoration five to eight months.

If you are already living in your R.O.S. and have no alternative but to stay during the restoration, it may be more difficult. I am not talking about minor projects now, but major ones. Even a kitchen job can be quite in-convenient if you are living there. A complete kitchen can be completed in a week and if you take proper precautions you won't find it too bad. For instance, seal the kitchen off from the rest of the house, even with plywood, if necessary, to keep dust and workmen from filtering through the rest of the house. Make arrangements to take your meals elsewhere. One room at a time restoration isn't too bad but the dust must be expected, even if that particular room is sealed off. And, of course, your personal possessions must be considered, from the standpoints of security and damage. With additions, make sure that the addition is as complete as possible before cutting the doorway into the existing structure. You can have it almost ready for carpet.

In a major restoration don't move in until it is completely finished. In many parts of the country you are wisely prevented from doing so by local building codes and inspectors. Aside from the dust, dirt, and lack of privacy, an incomplete project can be very unsafe. Electrical fires and shocks are probably the greatest hazard. Also, open stairways and missing railings can present potential hazards. You will also finish all the last odds and ends more quickly if there aren't the encumbrances of people and their possessions. But as always, let your own circumstances and common sense prevail.

CHAPTER 13

Cost Estimating

BELOW IS A list of items for estimating costs you may encounter in any restoration project. This list includes items for projects ranging from painting a room to a total restoration or rehabilitation, including additions. Some will not pertain to your particular project. Estimated costs may be five percent or less of actual cost.

In some areas of the country, costs by some trades may vary significantly. You may want to call several different subcontractors to verify that costs you are quoted are in line. Don't be discouraged if a few are higher. That situation exists everywhere. Some charge, and get, exorbitant prices. See Chapter 4 for estimated versus actual cost.

List of All Possible Costs for Total Renovation

	Estimated Cost	Actual Cost
1. Inspection fees ....$		$
2. Design assistance ....$		$
3. Loan closing costs ....$		$
4. Construction or short-term loan interest ....$		$
5. Fire insurance.............$		$
6. Temporary utilities ....$		$
7. Cleaning the R.O.S........$		$
8. Plans & specifications .....$		$
9. Permits & fees ....$		$
10. Clearing, grading & excavation for additions ......$		$

	Estimated Cost	Actual Cost
11. Footings ....$		$
12. Foundations ....$		$
13. Waterproofing ....$		$
14. Tearing out ....$		$
a. exterior walls ....$		$
b. interior walls ....$		$
c. roof shingles...........$		$
d. roof rafters ....$		$
e. plaster, drywall ....$		$
f. furnace, radiators ....$		$
g. plumbing ....$		$
h. electrical wiring, etc......$		$
i. total gutting............$		$
15. New framing — lumber, materials, & labor ....$		$
a. walls ....$		$
b. floors ....$		$
c. ceilings ....$		$
d. roof...................$		$
e. additions ....$		$
16. Steel ....$		$
17. Windows ....$		$
18. Exterior doors ....$		$
19. Roofing — labor & materials ....$		$
20. Concrete flatwork ....$		$
21. Exterior trim — labor & materials ....$		$
22. Exterior siding or veneers...$		$

	Estimated Cost	Actual Cost
23. Plumbing — upfitting	$	$
a. toilets	$	$
b. bath sinks	$	$
c. kitchen sinks	$	$
d. tubs, refinished	$	$
e. tubs, replaced	$	$
f. water heater	$	$
g. water pipes	$	$
24. Plumbing — new	$	$
a. kitchen(s)	$	$
b. bath(s)	$	$
25. Heating and A/C	$	$
26. Electrical — upfitting	$	$
27. Electrical — new wiring & service	$	$
28. Insulation	$	$
29. Drywall	$	$
30. Plaster	$	$
31. Water & sewer main repair	$	$
32. Well & septic system	$	$
33. Cabinets, bath vanities	$	$
34. Interior trim materials	$	$
35. Interior doors	$	$
36. Interior trim labor	$	$
37. Painting, interior	$	$
38. Painting, exterior	$	$
39. Appliances	$	$
40. Light fixtures	$	$
41. Floor coverings	$	$
42. Drives, walks, patios	$	$
43. Cleaning	$	$
44. Gutters, screens, miscellaneous	$	$
45. Wallpaper	$	$
46. Hardware & bath accessories	$	$
47. Landscaping	$	$
48. Miscellaneous allowance	$	$

Item-by-Item Estimating

1. Inspection fees. These costs will vary with locality and time involved. A quick phone call will get you an exact cost.

2. Design assistance. Whether you use an architect or a designer, I'd figure costs for approximately four to six hours. This charge does not include the cost of plans and specifications and assumes there is no supervision service included in the charge for plans and specs. It is for additional technical and design advice before and during the project that may or may not be needed.

3. Loan closing costs. These are charges collected by your lender and include their service charges for making the loan, *title insurance,* prepaid taxes, *recording fees,* and possibly other charges. You can get an exact quote of all charges prior to closing. I advise you to do so. Since the charges are generally based on a percentage of the amount you borrow, that amount reflects the size of your R.O.S.

4. Construction loan interest. As earlier discussed, loan interest is a cost of construction and should be treated as such, whether paid on a true construction loan that will be part of the permanent note or on a short-term personal note that will be *rolled over* into a new loan when the project is done. Project cost is usually related to the size of your R.O.S. and the time to complete renovation. An estimate can be obtained in advance from your lender. If you use your own money, you can record here the amount of interest you would have earned if you had invested this money otherwise.

5. Fire insurance. The amount carried is equal to the value of the completed R.O.S. The rate is also a function of size. An exact figure can be obtained from your insurance agent.

6. Temporary utilities. If there is no electricity or water available at the R.O.S., you will have to make arrangements for these utilities as discussed. Portable sanitation units also fall into this category. The highest cost will be for the sanitation unit, so the sooner you can ready the plumbing in your R.O.S., the sooner you can eliminate this cost.

7. Cleaning the R.O.S. Before you start renovating, cleaning is an important job. This is sometimes a job that you can do, but if not you can get an exact quote from a professional service listed in the Yellow Pages.

8. Plans and Specifications. An exact quote can and should be obtained very early in the game from your architect/designer.

9. Permits and fees. These are paid to local government agencies. You can get a quote over the phone.

10. Clearing, grading and excavation. An exact quote can be asked for beforehand, with a basement and without a basement.

11. Footings. This includes digging the trenches, if necessary forming *re bars,* purchasing the concrete and pouring it. It is based on an average 8' x 16" x 8" footing and does not include removal of old footings or jacking a wall up in order to place a footing under it. Those two items would have to be priced by getting quotes from the appropriate sub.

12. Foundation. Cost doesn't include demolition of existing walls to be rebuilt. It does include all materials — block, brick, stone, sand, mortar, *Durawall* — and all labor. For double walls, double the estimate. If you can't determine proper square footage, have your designer, or supplier do so (free!). Some brick, block, or stone masons will give a contract price, others will charge by the brick or block. Stone masons generally charge by the square foot.

13. Waterproofing. Use professionals!

14. Tearing out. Get prices for removal of and hauling away each item.

a. Exterior walls . . . . $ ln. ft.
b. Interior walls . . . . $ ln. ft.
c. Roof shingles . . . . $ sq. ft.
d. Roof rafters . . . . $ sq. ft.
e. Remove plaster . . . . $ sq. ft.
    drywall . . . . $ sq. ft.
f. Furnace, radiators . . . . $
g. Plumbing . . . . $
h. Electrical . . . . $

15. Framing — lumber, materials and labor.
a. Walls . . . . $ sq. ft.
b. Floors . . . . $ sq. ft.
c. Ceilings . . . . $ sq. ft.
d. Roofs . . . . $ sq. ft.
e. Additions . . . . $ sq. ft.

16. Steel. It is used where there is a large span or serious sag.

17. Windows. Include installation. This is for *insulated glass*, window grids if any, sash locks, and screens. You can find them for less and you can find them for more. Special windows, such as bay windows, will need to be quoted for unit price from the supplier and possibly installation price from your carpenter.

18. Exterior doors. Double for French doors, somewhere in between for aluminum sliding glass doors, and slightly higher for wood sliding glass doors. This cost should allow for installation of pre-hung units and weatherstripping, but not hardware other than hinges.

19. Roofing — labor and materials. Figure for standard weight 245-pound asphalt or fiberglass shingles, labor included. A square of shingles equals 100 square feet of roof area. For removal and hauling off of old layers, double the labor charge. For *built up* slate, shake, or metal, get an exact quote from the supplier and subcontractor.

20. Concrete flatwork. These are slabs used on garage and basement floors where concrete is to be finished smooth. It also involves use of insulating and reinforcing materials as required by municipal codes.

21. Exterior trim. These are the materials, including: soffit, fascia board, *soffit vents*, window and door moldings, and posts. Different houses will require different items, and a list of them can be made by a supplier or designer and an exact cost predetermined. If it all doesn't

need replacing, reduce accordingly. This will be a guess-timate.

22. Exterior siding or veneers. (For brick, block or stone, see foundations.) Figure wood, labor, and materials. Other sidings, such as vinyl or aluminum, will need to be quoted by a supplier or subcontractor.

23. Plumbing — upfitting. Figure fixture costs and labor.

a. Toilets . . . . $
b. Bath sinks . . . . $
c. Kitchen sinks . . . . $
d. Tubs refinished . . . . $
e. Tubs replaced . . . . $ (cast iron)
    . . . . $ (fiberglass)
f. Water heater . . . . $ (electric —
                         double for gas)
g. All waterpipes . . . . $

24. Plumbing/new. This will include all plumbing, fixtures, and installation (except those kitchen items that are considered appliances such as dishwasher, disposal) where the cost of plumbing them only is included. Relatively little plaster or drywall needs to be cut out for full plumbing restoration. Patching is therefore relatively easy.

25. Heating and A/C. This includes all new *ductwork*, *furnace(s)*, *compressor(s)*, and *thermostats*. Heatpump systems cost a little more to buy but are less expensive to install. Gas, oil, or electric without A/C is less expensive. Heatpumps have A/C as an intricate part of their operation so you get A/C automatically. Oil or gas boilers for water systems should be quoted on an individual basis. Central A/C added to these systems would be a total extra, the cost of a complete heat-A/C system. Exact quotes on any and all systems can be asked for very early in the game. Vent quotes for bath exhaust, dryer exhaust, and range ventilation do not include the fan, your electrician handles that. (Be sure all vents are vented to the outside and not to attics, basements, garages, or crawl spaces.)

26. Electrical — upfitting.

For wiring only to
    add dishwasher . . . . $
    add water heater . . . . $
    add receptacles (110 volt) . . . . $
    add switches . . . . $
    increase service for heavier loads, with
       circuit breakers (200 amp.) . . . . $
    add A/C only . . . . $
    add heat pump . . . . $

Costs should include all materials and labor, including average linear footage of all copper wire needed, *fished through existing walls*. For any other items get an exact quote.

27. Electrical — new. For all new switches; receptacles; circuit panels and breakers; wiring of all built-in appliances including water heater, furnaces and A/C; and wiring of all bath fans (cost of fans is under light fixtures). An exact quote based on your blueprints can be obtained from an electrician. Total new wiring can be done without removing all the plaster or drywall. A few cuts or holes in each wall may have to be made, but patching is relatively easy.

28. Insulation. For your needs, which may vary with climate, consult an insulation contractor and your local utilities.

29. Drywall. Quotes for a complete job can be obtained from a drywall sub.

30. Plaster
- a. patch only ....$ sq. ft.
- b. large areas ....$ sq. ft.
- c. Complete R.O.S.............$ sq. ft.

31. Water and sewer main repair. If these systems are fifty or more years old, replace them as soon as feasible.

32. Well and septic system. Where water and sewer are not available, and where conditions permit, obtain a firm quote for both.

Note: Most well drillers can give a contract price, especially if they are familiar with the area. Shop carefully. Try to avoid a per foot drilling charge. Be sure the well and its water meet local codes and health department requirements before paying for it.

Septic systems will vary by local requirements. Bedrooms determine the number of people living in the structure and thus how large the system, and price, should be. Again, be sure the system meets all codes and has been inspected before paying. If your locale doesn't have a building inspection department or health department inspector for either well or septic systems, consult your inspection engineer. He or she is qualified to inspect and any small additional charge is well worth it.

33. Cabinets, bath vanities. An exact quote can be given by your supplier; price will vary drastically. An average kitchen will have 12 to 15 feet of cabinets. Cabinet quotes should include labor to install and should be for a finished (painted or stained) product, including all hardware per linear foot.

34. Interior trim materials. Cost for trim is per linear foot of each room.

35. Interior doors.
- a. solid wood, prehung with casing
  — 2′6″ .... $
- b. hollow core hardwood, with casing
  — 2′6″ .... $
- c. hollow birch door, with casing
  — 2′6″ .... $

36. Interior trim labor. Labor includes applying standard trim and hanging all doors.

37. Painting, interior. Including all materials and two coats of paint. Exact quote from the painter may be obtained, using the plans.

38. Painting, exterior. Including all materials and *caulking* of all seams and joints, exterior painting, (even for a brick or stone veneer), sanding, and scraping. Exact quote from the painter may be obtained, using the plans.

39. Appliances. Costs will vary widely by brand and quality.

40. Light fixtures. The sky's the limit. Quotes from light fixture suppliers can be taken from your plans. Most old existing fixtures in an O.S. can be considered unsafe and should be repaired or replaced. Repairs should be made by an Underwriters Laboratories (U.L.) approved technician listed in the Yellow Pages. Local codes may require this.

41. Floor coverings.

42. Drives, walks, patios.

43. Cleaning. Same as #7, but this time more thorough, including windows.

44. Gutters, screens, miscellaneous. Miscellaneous is anything not specifically planned for and items, such as garage doors, should be accounted for.

45. Wallpaper. This is a non-necessity, but most builders give their customers a dollar allowance installed. Why not use that?

46. Hardware and bath accessories.

47. Landscaping.

48. Miscellaneous allowance. Figure five percent of the total cost.

Ballpark Estimating

Obviously completing all forty-eight items of estimating will take some time and effort on your part and it's not feasible to do it for every R.O.S. you look at, only when you get close to buying a particular one. So what do you do to enable you to estimate quickly when you are in your seach for your R.O.S.? You use "ballpark figures" to aid you in your decision-making process. It is not very accurate, but accurate enough to decide whether you should take the time to do a cost estimate on it. This procedure concerns itself with the basics and the major costs in restoration. Remember to figure cost per square foot.

1. Total gut and restoration — all you have is four walls, floor and ceiling joints, roof that needs repair, and a fairly sound structure when youre done.
2. New kitchen — (average size) complete, including tearing out.
3. New bath — each, complete and including gutting.
4. New roof.
5. Repair plaster — in fairly good condition **or** cover plaster with drywall.
6. Paint — complete.
7. New electrical — complete.
8. New heat — A/C.
9. Insulation.
10. Extensive carpentry.

CHAPTER 14

Tearing Down and Rebuilding

Tearing Down

The following is the general order of steps and the approximate time for the completion of the tearing down phase of a renovation project.

Wall Removal

For renovations the first step is wall removal, per your master plan and blueprints. If only a few walls are to be removed, your carpenters can usually handle first the removal of the plaster or wallboard for those walls only. If all the plaster is to be removed from all the walls, remove the plaster before tearing out any walls. Your carpenter may want to hold off on wall removal until ready to do any additional framing or bracing. This is fine. Discuss this scheduling, as well as costs, in the planning stage.

Plaster Removal

Other than cutting holes to change wiring or plumbing, I recommend removing plaster only if it is severely cracked or falling down. Patching is always cheaper — even covering cracked walls with drywall is less expensive than total gutting. Keep in mind that all interior trim must be removed, and can seldom be saved, in total gutting. Allow one-half to one day per room, including trim removal.

As mentioned in estimating, plumbing removal may necessitate removing some plaster, but usually in small areas that can easily be patched. Time will vary with the difficulty of the job and the extent of work to be done, but one to two days should suffice.

Wiring and Plumbing Removal

If you are doing a total gut and have removed all the plaster or drywall, then this is the time for removing any plumbing pipes, electrical wiring, radiator pipes, or boilers you have decided to replace. All this can generally be done in one week.

For New Additions

Clearing, grading, excavation, and hauling away trash are the first steps for new additions. Allow one to three days.

Protection From Weather and Vandals

You must protect what you already have in your O.S. from the elements and vandals. Have your carpenter install temporary locks and board up missing windows. If the roof is in serious disrepair, it should be among the first items rebuilt, but at least cover it with plastic for now. Water can do more damage than vandals.

Rebuilding

The following is the general order of steps and the approximate time for completion of the rebuilding phase of a renovation project.

Foundation, Concrete, and Brick Work

Adding or repairing footings and foundations, slab work in basements, and such brick work as chimneys, new foundations or other brick repairs is best done after all the removal is completed. The only exception is the roof, which I will discuss momentarily. Allow one week for repair or additions of footings and foundations.

If your inspection engineer has reported or if there is evidence that water is or has been in the basement or crawl space, now is the time to call in your waterproofing subcontractor. Both can be waterproofed from the inside, but it is best to do it from the outside. This often requires digging around the foundation and can be expensive, so be sure to get bids. A footing drain may be required and your waterproofing sub is responsible for this. Seek additional advice or opinions, if needed, from your architect, inspection engineer, or building inspector.

Rough Carpentry

By now you understand that your carpenter is one of your key people, and is needed from the onset of the project for plan review through the initial stages of restoration. This is the time to remedy all sags. Sags should always be corrected prior to doing any new plumbing because correcting sags can crack pipes.

It is wise to have your carpenter ask the electrician, plumber, and heating/air-conditioning subs what can be done to make their jobs easier. For example, many old houses have receptacles in the baseboards. Removal of the baseboard facilitates replacement of wiring, but the baseboard removal is a job usually handled by your carpenter. The same is true with the removal of kitchen cabinets to aid the plumber. *Chases* may need to be constructed for pipes, heat vents, A/C lines, and service wires. This is accomplished by *furring out* a wall, or building a box-like run from floor to ceiling in closets, or wall-to-wall along the ceiling at an inconspicuous place. These chases or furred areas may or may not be indicated on the plans. If they are not, your subs can work it out on the job.

Carpentry rough-work will vary with the complexity and extent of restoration but allow a maximum of three weeks.

Roofing

As mentioned earlier, you should have your roof repaired as soon as possible to prevent further deterioration of the O.S. With additions, the roofing is completed early on for the same reason. Also, with the roof repaired your other subs can work inside on other phases regardless of the weather.

Your carpenter will repair any rotten or sagging roof framing and your roofing sub will then install new roofing or patch existing roofing per your specifications. The time it will take to complete roofing is from one day to two weeks, weather permitting.

Note: If there is to be chimney repair, or one to be added, and you are putting on new roofing, have the roofer leave undone an area adjacent to the chimney. This will prevent damage to the new material while the chimney work progresses. Hold back 10 percent of the roofer's contract amount until the roof is completed.

Electrical, Plumbing, Heat-A/C

All your electrical, plumbing, and heat-A/C should be completed at this time, prior to insulation of side walls. Time to complete all three: two to three weeks.

Note: Don't change the pipes, unless you do not have good water pressure. You can change them later if necessary with little damage to existing walls. The same applies to electrical work. If existing electrical service is adequate for most of the house, don't remove it unless you are doing a full gut. You can add to it as added electrical demand requires. Of course if it is deemed unsafe, remove it.

Chimney

Chimneys can now be added or repaired. Old chimneys, if they are structurally sound (see your inspection engineer's report), should be relined with terra-cotta flue liners and new dampers, if this was deemed necessary when they were inspected. This is faster and less expensive than completely rebuilding. Time to repair: two days to one week. Time to build new: one to two weeks not including tearing down old chimneys, which could take one day to one week.

Exterior Siding and Trim

This phase can be completed even while your electrical, plumbing, and heating and air work is being done inside. Time to complete is one to three weeks.

Insulation

The cost of energy is high and sure to go higher, so it pays to insulate well. You not only save on energy bills in the long run, you get immediate savings because you can install a smaller heating and cooling system that will cost less. Virtually every structure can be insulated without removing the inside walls. This is accomplished by drilling small holes in exterior walls from the outside and blowing fiberglass or cellulose insulation through the hole into the wall cavity. The hole is then plugged. The alternative is removal of the interior plaster or drywall of all exterior walls to install insulation batting. This obviously is quite expensive unless you are doing a full gut anyway. Blowing the insulation into the wall cavities should provide adequate insulation for most climates, and a reputable firm should do the job neatly. You will not, however, have the *vapor barrier* that you would get with insulation from inside. You can compensate for this by painting all exterior walls with a vapor-barrier paint. Check local suppliers for types available in your area. Vapor barriers are important because moisture can escape through the walls, lessen the effectiveness of the insulation, and rot the framing. Before the insulation was added there was no such problem because the moisture could escape through the walls to the outside. Now it can't, so the object is to keep it inside the heated area. This also adds to your comfort, as moist air is more comfortable than dry air.

Be sure attic areas, crawl spaces, and basements are insulated as well as you can afford. Your utility companies can provide you with information on the amount of insulation needed for lowest rates and greatest savings. Time to complete is one to two weeks.

Drywall or Plaster

Now you are ready for installation or patching of plaster or drywall. Where possible, use drywall as a replacement for missing plaster or to cover cracked plaster. It is far less expensive and looks better. For your first project, try to find a drywall sub who supplies all materials and removes all trash. Plasterers always supply materials. In the winter you will need temporary heat not only to protect the plumbing, but to help speed the drywall or plastering job and prevent cracking caused by freezing — drywall mud or filler, and plaster, have a water base. Time to complete is two to four weeks.

Prime Painting

I find it beneficial to prime the walls (apply the first coat of paint) as soon as the plaster or drywall sub is finished. Imperfections in the wall show up after priming and serious flaws can be corrected now or later. Discuss that with your drywall or plaster sub beforehand.

If there is no stained woodwork, the walls can be spray painted, which is faster and less expensive than using brushes and rollers. Prime painting by spraying can usually be completed in one day, even for a rather large R.O.S. If you have quite a bit of stained woodwork and molding, brushes and rollers would be used and stained areas must be masked to prevent their getting splattered.

This would take one to two weeks and could be delayed until after any interior trim is added or repaired.

Interior Trim

Interior doors, trims, and moldings are repaired, replaced, or added at this time and new cabinets, if any, for your kitchen and baths installed. Allow one to two weeks.

Painting

You are now ready for interior as well as exterior painting, although exterior painting could be completed earlier — right after exterior trim. That should be discussed and worked out with your painting sub. It is usually easier to complete the whole job at one time. Painting inside and outside will take two to three weeks.

Final Trims

At this time you are ready to install any Formica, vinyl flooring, plumbing fixtures, electrical trims, light fixtures, and final trim for heating and air-conditioning — in that order. Allow one to two weeks.

If you are finishing or refinishing hardwood floors, I recommend you wait until all the above is completed and have the floors done just prior to laying any carpeting. Allow three days for sanding, staining and sealing hardwood floors. You are now ready for carpeting and wallpaper, the last items other than cleanup. (You can reverse carpeting and cleanup.) Allow one week.

Cleanup

With final cleanup also comes trash removal, which should take only a few hours, or one day, maximum. At this point you can complete any necessary landscaping.

Final Inspection and Loan Closing

When all is done, be sure your subs have called for their final inspections and that you have called for a final building inspection. Again, if you don't have a building-inspection department, for peace of mind, call in an inspection engineer before final payment to relevant subs. Final inspections will verify compliance with codes and that everything works.

When all has been approved by inspectors, utility companies (if applicable), your lender, and most importantly *you*, you are ready to convert any construction financing to the permanent mortgage. This is usually arranged at the convenience of the lender, attorney, and you. It takes less than an hour.

Now you can move in and enjoy.

Appendix

The following legal instruments are published as examples. Because of varying state laws, these should not be used by you unless such use is approved by your attorney.

MANAGER'S CONSTRUCTION CONTRACT

1. General

This contract dated _____ is between _____ (OWNER) and _____ (MANAGER), and provides for supervision of construction by MANAGER of a residence to be built on OWNER'S Property at ____ , _____ and described as _____ . The project is described on drawings dated _____ and specifications dated ____ _____ , which documents are a part hereof.

2. Schedule

The project is to start as near as possible to _____ , with anticipated completion _____ months from starting date.

3. Contract Fee and Payment

3A. OWNER agrees to pay MANAGER a minimum fee of _____ ($) for the work performed under this contract, said fee to be paid in installments as the work progresses as follows:

a. Down payment — due prior to start of work	$ _____
b. Framed	$ _____
c. Roof on	$ _____
d. Ready for drywall	$ _____
e. Trimmed out	$ _____
f. Final	$ _____

3B. Payments billed by MANAGER are due in full within ten (10) days of bill mailing date.

3C. Final payment to MANAGER is due in full upon completion of residence; however, MANAGER may bill upon "Substantial completion" (see paragraph 11.0 for the definition of terms) the amount of the final payment less X percent of the value of work yet outstanding. In such a case, the amount of the fee withheld will be billed upon completion.

4. General Intent of Contract

It is intended that the OWNER be in effect his or her own "General Contractor" and that the MANAGER provide the OWNER with expert guidance and advice, and supervision and coordination of trades and material delivery. It is agreed that MANAGER acts in a professional capacity and simply as agent for OWNER, and that as such he or she shall not assume or incur any pecuniary responsibility to contractor, subcontractors, laborers or material suppliers. OWNER will contract directly with subcontractors, obtain from them their certificates of insurance and release of liens. Similarly, OWNER will open own accounts with material suppliers and be billed and pay directly for materials supplied. OWNER shall pay all expenses incurred in completing the project, except MANAGER'S overhead as specifically exempted in Paragraph 9. In fulfilling his or her responsibilities to OWNER, MANAGER shall perform at all times in a manner intended to be beneficial to the interests of the OWNER.

5. Responsibilities of Manager

General

MANAGER shall have full responsibility for coordination of trades, ordering materials and scheduling of work, correction of errors and conflicts, if any, in the work, materials, or plans, compliance with applicable codes, judgment as to the adequacy of trades' work to meet standards specified, together with any other function that might reasonably be expected in order to provide OWNER with a single source of responsibility for supervision and coordination of work.

Specific Responsibilities

1. Submit to OWNER in a timely manner a list of subcontractors and suppliers MANAGER believes competent to perform the work at competitive prices. OWNER may use such recommendations or not.
2. Submit to OWNER a list of items requiring OWNER'S selection, with schedule dates for selection indicated, and recommended sources indicated.
3. Obtain in OWNER'S name(s) all permits required by governmental authorities.
4. Arrange for all required surveys and site engineering work.
5. Arrange for all the installation of temporary services.
6. Arrange for and supervise clearing, disposal of stumps and brush, and all excavating and grading work.
7. Develop material lists and order all materials in a timely manner, from sources designated by OWNER.
8. Schedule, coordinate, and supervise the work for all subcontractors designated by OWNER.
9. Review, when requested by OWNER, questionable bills and recommend payment action to OWNER.
10. Arrange for common labor for hand digging, grading, and cleanup during construction, and for disposal of construction waste.
11. Supervise the project through completion, as defined in Paragraph 11.

6. Responsibilities of Owner

OWNER agrees to:

1. Arrange all financing needed for project, so that sufficient funds exist to pay all bills within ten (10) days of their presentation.
2. Select subcontractors and suppliers in a timely manner so as not to delay the work. Establish charge accounts and execute contracts with same, as appropriate, and inform MANAGER of accounts opened and of MANAGER'S authority in using said accounts.
3. Select items requiring OWNER selection, and inform MANAGER of selections and sources on or before date shown on selection list.

Continued on page 66

4. Inform MANAGER promptly of any changes desired or other matters affecting schedule so that adjustments can be incorporated in the schedule.

5. Appoint an agent to pay for work and make decisions to OWNER'S behalf in cases where OWNER is unavailable to do so.

6. Assume complete responsibility for any theft and vandalism of OWNER'S property occurring on the job. Authorize replacement/repairs required in a timely manner.

7. Provide a surety bond for lender if required.

8. Obtain release of liens documentation as required by OWNER'S lender.

9. Provide insurance coverage as listed in Paragraph 12.

10. Pay promptly for all work done, materials used, and other services and fees generated in the execution of the project, except as specifically exempted in Paragraph 9.

7. Exclusions

The following items shown on the drawings and/or specifications are NOT included in this contract, insofar as MANAGER supervision responsibilities are concerned:

(List below)

8. Extras/Changes

MANAGER'S fee is based on supervising the project as defined in the drawings and specifications. Should additional supervisory work be required because of EXTRAS or CHANGES occasioned by OWNER, unforeseen site conditions, or governmental authorities, MANAGER will be paid an additional fee of X percent of cost of such work. Since the basic contract fee is a *minimum fee*, no downward adjustment will be made if the scope of work is reduced, unless contract is cancelled in accordance with Paragraphs 14 or 15.

9. Manager's Facilities

MANAGER will furnish own transportation and office facilities for MANAGER'S use in supervising the project at no expense to OWNER. MANAGER shall provide general liability and workmen's compensation insurance coverage for MANAGER'S direct employees only at no cost to OWNER.

10. Use of Manager's Accounts

MANAGER may have certain "trade" accounts not available to OWNER which OWNER may find it to his or her advantage to utilize. If MANAGER is billed and pays such accounts from MANAGER'S resources, OWNER will reimburse MANAGER within ten (10) days of receipt of MANAGER'S bill at cost plus X percent of such materials/services.

11. Project Completion

    a. The project shall be deemed completed when all the terms of this contract have been fulfilled, and a Residential Use Permit has been issued.

    b. The project shall be deemed "substantially complete" when a Residential Use Permit has been issued, and less than   Dollars ($) of work remains to be done.

12. Insurance

OWNER shall insure that workmen's compensation and general liability insurance are provided to protect all parties of interest and shall hold MANAGER harmless from all claims by subcontractors, suppliers and their personnel, and for personnel arranged for by MANAGER in OWNER'S behalf, if any.

OWNER shall maintain fire and extended coverage insurance sufficient to provide 100 percent coverage of project value at all stages of construction, and MANAGER shall be named in the policy to insure his or her interest in the project.

Continued on page 67

Should OWNER or MANAGER determine that certain subcontractors, laborers, or suppliers are not adequately covered by general liability or workmen's compensation insurance to protect OWNER'S and/or MANAGER'S interests, MANAGER may, as agent of OWNER, cover said personnel on MANAGER'S policies, and OWNER shall reimburse MANAGER for the premium at cost plus X percent.

13. Manager's Right to Terminate Contract

Should the work be stopped by any public authority for a period of thirty (30) days or more through no fault of the MANAGER, or should work be stopped through act or neglect of OWNER for ten (10) days or more, or should OWNER fail to pay MANAGER any payment due within ten (10) days written notice to OWNER, MANAGER may stop work and/or terminate this contract and recover from OWNER payment for all work completed as a proration of the total contract sum, plus X percent of the fee remaining to be paid if the contract were completed as liquidated damages.

14. Owner's Right to Terminate Contract

Should the work be stopped or wrongly prosecuted through act or neglect of MANAGER for ten (10) days or more, OWNER may so notify MANAGER in writing. If work is not properly resumed within ten (10) days of such notice, OWNER may terminate this contract. Upon termination, entire balance then due MANAGER for that percentage of work then completed, as a proration of the total contract sum, shall be due and payable and all further liabilities of MANAGER under this contract shall cease. Balance due to MANAGER shall take into account any additional cost to OWNER to complete the house occasioned by MANAGER.

15. Manager/Owner's Liability for Collection
Expenses

Should MANAGER or OWNER respectively be required to collect funds rightfully due him or her through legal proceedings, MANAGER or OWNER respectively agrees to pay all costs and reasonable Attorney's fees.

16. Warranties and Service

MANAGER warrants that he or she will supervise the construction in accordance with the terms of this contract. No other warranty by MANAGER is implied or exists.

Subcontractors normally warrant their work for one year, and some manufacturers supply yearly warranties on certain of their equipment; such warranties shall run to the OWNER and the enforcement of these warranties is in all cases the responsibility of the OWNER and not the MANAGER.

(MANAGER) _____ (seal) Date: _____

(OWNER) _____ (seal) Date: _____

(OWNER) _____ (seal) Date: _____

CONTRACT TO BUILD HOUSE
(Cost Plus Fee)

Contractor: _____

Owner: _____ Date: _____

    Owner is or shall become fee simple owner of a tract or parcel of land known or described as: _____ .

    Contractor hereby agrees to construct a residence on the above described lot according to the plans and specifications identified as: Exhibit A — plans and specifications drawn _____ by

_____ .

    Owner shall pay Contractor for the construction of said house cost of construction and a fee of _____ .

Cost is estimated in Exhibit B. Each item in Exhibit B is an estimate and is not to be construed as an exact cost.

    Owner shall secure/has secured financing for the construction of said house in the amount of cost plus fee, which shall be disbursed by a savings and loan or bank from time to time as construction progresses, subject to a holdback of no more than X percent. Owner hereby authorizes Contractor to submit a request for draws in the name of Owner under such loan up to the percentage completion of construction and to accept said draws in partial payment hereof. In addition, it is understood that the Contractor's fee shall be paid in installments by the savings and loan or bank at the time of and as a part of each construction draw as a percentage of completion, so that the entire fee shall be paid at or before the final construction draw.

    Contractor shall commence construction as soon as feasible after closing of the construction loan and shall pursue work to a scheduled completion on or before X months from commencement, except if such completion shall be delayed by unusually unfavorable weather, strikes, natural disasters, unavailability of labor or materials, or changes in the plans or specifications.

    Contractor shall build the residence in substantial compliance with the plans and specifications and in a good and workmanlike manner, and shall meet all building codes. Contractor shall not be responsible for failure of materials or equipment not Contractor's fault. Except as herein set out, Contractor shall make no representations or warranties with respect to the work to be done hereunder.

    Owner shall not occupy the residence and Contractor shall hold the keys until all work has been completed and all monies due Contractor hereunder shall have been paid.

    Owner shall not make changes to the plans or specifications until such changes shall be evidenced in writing, the costs, if any, of such changes shall be set out, and the construction lender and Contractor shall have approved such changes. Any additional costs thereof shall be paid in advance, or payment guaranteed in advance of the work being accomplished.

    Contractor shall not be obligated to continue work hereunder in the event Owner shall breach any term or condition hereof, or if for any reason the construction lender shall cease making advances under the construction loan upon proper request thereof.

    Any additional or special stipulations attached hereto and signed by the parties shall be and are made a part hereof.

Owner: _____ (seal)

        _____ (seal)

Contractor: _____ (seal)

CONTRACT TO BUILD HOUSE
(Contract Bid)

Contractor: _____

Owner: _____ Date: _____

    Owner is or shall become fee simple owner of a tract or parcel of land known or described as: _____ .

    Contractor hereby agrees to construct a residence on the above described lot according to the plans drawn by _____ , and the specifications herein attached.

    Owner shall pay Contractor for the construction of said house $ _____ .

    Prior to commencement hereunder, owner shall secure financing for the construction of said house in the amount of $ _____ , which loan shall be disbursed from time to time as construction progresses, subject to a holdback of no more than X percent. Owner hereby authorizes Contractor to submit a request for draws in the name of the Owner from the savings and loan, or similar institution, up to the percentage completion of construction and to accept said draws in partial payment thereof.

    Contractor shall commence construction as soon as feasible after closing and shall pursue work to a scheduled completion on or before X months from commencement, except if such completion shall be delayed by unusually unfavorable weather, strikes, natural disasters, unavailability of labor or materials, or changes in the plans and specifications.

    Contractor shall build the residence in substantial compliance with the plans and specifications and in a good and workmanlike manner, and shall meet all building code requirements. Contractor shall not be responsible for failure of materials or equipment not Contractor's fault. Except as herein set out, Contractor shall make no representations or warranties with respect to the work to be done hereunder.

    Owner shall not occupy the residence and Contractor shall hold the keys until all work has been completed and all monies due Contractor hereunder shall have been paid.

    Owner shall not make any changes to the plans and specifications until such changes shall be evidenced in writing, the costs, if any, of such changes shall be set out, and any additional costs thereof shall be paid in advance of the work being accomplished.

    Contractor shall not be obligated to continue work hereunder in the event Owner shall breach any term or condition hereof, or if for any reason the construction draws shall cease to be advanced upon proper request thereof.

    Any additional or special stipulations attached hereto and signed by the parties shall be and are made a part hereof.

Contractor: _____ (seal)

Owner: _____ (seal)

             _____ (seal)

SCHEDULE OF MATERIALS

☐ Proposed Construction   No. _____
                                 (To be inserted by FHA or VA)
☐ Under Construction

Property address _____ City _____ State _____

Mortgagor or Sponsor _____   _____
                              (Name)   (Address)

Contractor or Builder_____   _____
                              (Name)   (Address)

INSTRUCTIONS

1. For additional information on how this form is to be submitted, number of copies, etc., see the instructions applicable to the FHA Application for Mortgage Insurance or VA Request for Determination of Reasonable Value, as the case may be.

2. Describe all materials and equipment to be used, whether or not shown on the drawings, by marking an X in each appropriate check-box and entering the information called for in each space. If space is inadequate, enter "See misc." and describe under item 27 or on an attached sheet. THE USE OF PAINT CONTAINING MORE THAN ONE PERCENT LEAD BY WEIGHT IS PROHIBITED.

3. Work not specifically described or shown will not be considered unless required, then the minimum acceptable will be assumed. Work exceeding minimum requirements cannot be considered unless specifically described.

4. Include no alternates, "or equal" phrases, or contradictory items. (Consideration of a request for acceptance of substitute materials or equipment is not thereby precluded.)

5. Include signatures required at the end of this form.

6. The construction shall be completed in compliance with the related drawings and specifications, as amended during processing. The specifications include this Description of Materials and the applicable Minimum Property Standards.

---

1. EXCAVATION:
Bearing soil, type _____

2. FOUNDATIONS:
Footings: concrete mix _____; strength psi _____   Reinforcing_____

Foundation wall: material _____   Reinforcing_____

Interior foundation wall: material _____   Party foundation wall _____

Columns: material and sizes _____   Piers: material and reinforcing _____

Girders: material and sizes _____   Sills: material_____

Basement entrance areaway _____   Window areaways _____

Waterproofing _____   Footing drains _____

Termite protection _____

Basementless space: ground cover _____; insulation _____;

   foundation vents _____

Special foundations_____

Additional information: _____

---

3. CHIMNEYS:
Material_____   Prefabricated (make and size)_____

Flue lining: material _____   Heater flue size_____

   Fireplace flue size_____

Continued on page 71

Vents *(material and size):* gas or oil heater _____; water heater _____
Additional information:_____

4. FIREPLACES:
Type: ☐ solid fuel; ☐ gas-burning; ☐ circulator *(make and size)*_____
Ash dump and clean-out _____
Fireplace: facing _____; lining _____; hearth _____; mantel _____
Additional information: _____

5. EXTERIOR WALLS:
Wood frame: wood grade, and species _____ ☐ Corner bracing.
　Building paper or felt _____
　Sheathing _____; thickness _____; width _____; ☐ solid;
　☐ spaced _____"o.c.; ☐ diagonal: _____
　Siding _____; grade _____; type _____; size _____;
　exposure _____"; fastening _____
　Shingles _____; grade _____; type _____; size _____;
　exposure _____"; fastening _____
　Stucco _____; thickness _____";
　Lath _____; weight _____lbs.
　Masonry veneer _____ Sills _____ Lintels _____ Base flashing _____
Masonry: ☐ solid ☐ faced ☐ stuccoed; total wall thickness _____";
　facing thickness _____"; facing material _____
　Backup material _____; thickness _____"; bonding _____
　Door sills _____ Window sills _____ Lintels _____ Base flashing _____
　Interior surfaces: dampproofing, _____ coats of _____; furring _____
Additional information: _____
Exterior painting: material _____; number of coats _____
Gable wall construction: ☐ same as main walls; ☐ other construction _____

6. FLOOR FRAMING:
Joists: wood, grade, and species _____; other _____;
　bridging _____; anchors _____
Concrete slab: ☐ basement floor; ☐ first floor; ☐ ground supported;
　☐ self-supporting; mix _____; thickness _____";
　reinforcing _____; insulation _____; membrane _____
Fill under slab: material _____; thickness _____".
Additional information: _____

7. SUBFLOORING: *(Describe underflooring for special floors under item 21.)*
Material: grade and species _____; size _____; type _____
Laid: ☐ first floor; ☐ second floor; ☐ attic _____ sq. ft.; ☐ diagonal; ☐ right angles.
Additional information: _____

8. FINISH FLOORING: *(Wood only.　Describe other finish flooring under item 21.)*

Location	Rooms	Grade	Species	Thickness	Width	Bldg. Paper	Finish
First floor							
Second floor							
Attic floor___ sq. ft.							
Additional information:							

9. PARTITION FRAMING:
Studs: wood, grade, and species _____ size and spacing _____
　Other _____
Additional information: _____

10. CEILING FRAMING:
Joists: wood, grade, and species _____
　Other _____ Bridging _____
Additional information: _____

Continued on page 72

Appendix

11. ROOF FRAMING:
    Rafters: wood, grade, and species _____
        Roof trusses (see detail): grade and species _____
    Additional information: _____

12. ROOFING:
    Sheathing: wood, grade and species _____ ☐ solid; ☐ spaced _____"o.c.
    Roofing _____; grade _____; size _____; type _____
    Underlay _____; weight or thickness_____;
        size _____; fastening _____
    Built-up roofing _____; number of plies _____;
        surfacing material _____
    Flashing: material _____; gage or weight _____;
        ☐ gravel stops; ☐ snow guards
    Additional information: _____

13. GUTTERS AND DOWNSPOUTS:
    Gutters: material _____; gage or weight _____; size _____; shape _____
    Downspouts: material _____; gage or weight _____;
        size _____; shape _____; number _____
    Downspouts connected to: ☐ Storm sewer; ☐ sanitary sewer; ☐ dry-well.
        ☐ Splash blocks: material and size _____
    Additional information: _____

14. LATH AND PLASTER:
    Lath ☐ walls, ☐ ceilings: material _____; weight or thickness_____
        Plaster: coats ____; finish _____
    Dry-wall ☐ walls, ☐ ceilings: material _____; thickness _____;
        finish_____
    Joint treatment _____

15. DECORATING: *(Paint, wallpaper, etc.)*

Rooms	Wall Finish Material and Application	Ceiling Finish Material and Application
Kitchen		
Bath		
Other		

    Additional information: _____

16. INTERIOR DOORS AND TRIM:
    Doors: type _____; material _____; thickness _____
    Door trim: type_____; material_____;
        Base: type _____; material _____; size _____
    Finish: doors _____; trim _____
    Other trim *(item, type and location)* _____
    Additional information: _____

17. WINDOWS:
    Windows: type_____; make_____;
        material _____; sash thickness _____
    Glass: grade _____; ☐ sash weights;
        ☐ balances, type _____; head flashing_____
    Trim: type _____; material _____
        Paint _____; number coats _____
    Weatherstripping: type _____; material _____;
        Storm sash, number_____

Continued on page 73

Screens: □ full; □ half: type_____; number _____;
    screen cloth material _____
Basement windows: type _____; material _____;
    screens, number _____; Storm sash, number _____
Special windows _____
Additional information: _____

18. ENTRANCES AND EXTERIOR DETAIL:
Main entrance door: material _____; width_____
    thickness_____".
Frame: material _____; thickness_____"
Other entrance doors: material _____; width_____
    thickness_____".
Frame: material _____; thickness_____"
Head flashing _____ Weatherstripping: type _____; saddles _____
Screen doors: thickness _____"; number _____
    screen cloth material _____
    Storm doors: thickness _____"; number _____
Combination storm and screen doors: thickness_____"; number _____;
    screen cloth material _____
Shutters: □ hinged; □ fixed. Railings _____, Attic louvers _____
Exterior millwork: grade and species _____
    Paint _____; number coats _____
Additional information: _____

19. CABINETS AND INTERIOR DETAIL:
Kitchen cabinets, wall units: material _____;
    lineal feet of shelves _____; shelf width _____
    Base units: material _____; counter top _____; edging _____
    Back and end splash _____ Finish of cabinets _____; number coats _____
Medicine cabinets: make _____; model _____
Other cabinets and built-in furniture _____
Additional information: _____

20. STAIRS:

Stair	Treads		Risers		Strings		Handrail		Balusters	
	Material	Thickness	Material	Thickness	Material	Size	Material	Size	Material	Size
Basement										
Main										
Attic										
Disappearing: make and model number										
Additional information:										

21. SPECIAL FLOORS AND WAINSCOT

Wainscot   Floors

Location	Material, Color, Border, Sizes, Gage, Etc.	Threshold Material	Wall Base Material	Underfloor Material
Kitchen				
Bath				

Location	Material, Color, Border, Cap, Sizes, Gage, Etc.	Height	Height Over Tub	Height in Showers (From Floor)
Bath				

Continued on page 74

Bathroom accessories: ☐ Recessed; material _____ ; number _____ ;

☐ Attached; material _____ ; number _____ .

Additional material: _____

22. PLUMBING:

Fixture	Number Location	Make	Mfr's Fixture Identification No.	Size	Color
Sink					
Lavatory					
Water closet					
Bathtub					
Shower over tub △					
Stall shower △					
Laundry trays					

△ Curtain rod   △ Door   ☐ Shower pan: material _____

Water supply: ☐ public; ☐ community system; ☐ individual (private) system.*

Sewage disposal: ☐ public; ☐ community system; ☐ individual (private) system.*

*Show and describe individual system in complete detail in separate drawings and specifications according to requirements.

House drain (inside): ☐ cast iron; ☐ tile; ☐ other _____

House sewer (outside): ☐ cast iron; ☐ tile; ☐ other _____

Water piping: ☐ galvanized steel; ☐ copper tubing;

☐ other _____ Sill cocks, number _____

Domestic water heater: type _____ ;

make and model _____ ; heating capacity _____ gph. 100° rise.

Storage tank: material _____ ; capacity _____ gallons.

Gas service: ☐ utility company; ☐ liq. pet. gas; ☐ other _____

Gas piping: ☐ cooking; ☐ house heating.

Footing drains connected to: ☐ storm sewer; ☐ sanitary sewer; ☐ dry well.

Sump pump; make and model _____

capacity _____ ; discharges into _____

23. HEATING:

☐ Hot water. ☐ Steam. ☐ Vapor. ☐ One-pipe system. ☐ Two-pipe system.

☐ Radiators. ☐ Convectors. ☐ Baseboard radiation.

Make and model _____

Radiant panel: ☐ floor; ☐ wall; ☐ ceiling.   Panel coil: material _____

☐ Circulator.   ☐ Return pump.   Make and model _____

_____ ; capacity _____ gpm.

Boiler: make and model _____

Output _____ Btuh; net rating _____ Btuh.

Additional information: _____

Warm air: ☐ Gravity.   ☐ Forced.   Type of system _____

Duct material: supply _____ ; return _____

Insulation _____ , thickness _____ ☐ Outside air intake.

Furnace: make and model _____

Input _____ Bthu.; Output _____ Btuh.

Continued on page 75

Additional information: _____
☐ Space heater; ☐ floor furnace; ☐ wall heater. Input _____ Btuh.;
    Output _____ Btuh.; number units _____
    Make, model _____
      Additional information: _____
Controls: make and types _____
Additional information: _____
Fuel: ☐ Coal; ☐ oil; ☐ gas; ☐ liq. pet. gas; ☐ electric;
    ☐ other _____; storage capacity _____
Additional information: _____
Firing equipment furnished separately: ☐ Gas burner, conversion type.
                         ☐ Stoker: hopper feed ☐; bin feed
    Oil burner: ☐ pressure atomizing; ☐ vaporizing _____
    Make and model _____ Control _____
Additional information: _____
Electric heating system: type _____
    Input _____ watts; @ _____ volts; Output _____ Btuh.
Additional information: _____
Ventilating equipment: attic fan, make and model _____;
    capacity _____ cfm.
    kitchen exhaust fan, make and model _____
Other heating, ventilating, or cooling equipment _____
_____

24. ELECTRIC WIRING:
Service: ☐ overhead; ☐ underground. Panel: ☐ fuse box; ☐ circuit-breaker;
    Make _____ AMP's _____ No. circuits _____
Wiring: ☐ conduit; ☐ armored cable; ☐ nonmetallic cable; ☐ knob and tube;
    ☐ Other _____
Special outlets: ☐ range; ☐ water heater; ☐ Other _____
☐ Doorbell. ☐ Chimes. ☐ Push-button locations _____
Additional information: _____

25. LIGHTING FIXTURES:
Total number of fixtures _____
Total allowance for fixtures, typical installation, $ _____
Nontypical installation _____
Additional information: _____

26. INSULATION:

Location	Thickness	Material, Type, and Method of Installation	Vapor Barrier
Roof			
Ceiling			
Wall			
Floor			

HARDWARE: *(make, material, and finish.)* _____
_____

SPECIAL EQUIPMENT: *(State material or make, model and quantity. Include only equipment and appliances which are acceptable by local law, custom and*

Continued on page 76

applicable FHA standards. Do not include items which, by established custom, are supplied by occupant and removed when he vacates premises or chattles prohibited by law from becoming realty.) _____

_____
_____
_____
_____
_____
_____
_____
_____

27. MISCELLANEOUS: *(Describe any main dwelling materials, equipment, or construction items not shown elsewhere; or use to provide additional information where the space provided was inadequate. Always reference by item number to correspond to numbering used on this form.)* _____

_____
_____
_____
_____
_____
_____
_____
_____
_____
_____
_____

PORCHES:

_____
_____
_____

TERRACES:

_____
_____
_____

GARAGES:

_____
_____
_____

WALKS AND DRIVEWAYS:
Driveway: width_____; base material_____"; thickness_____"
    surfacing material_____; thickness _____"
Front walk: width_____; material _____; thickness_____".
Service walk: width_____; material _____; thickness_____".
Steps: material _____; treads_____"; risers_____".
Cheek walls_____

OTHER ONSITE IMPROVEMENTS:
(Specify all exterior onsite improvements not described elsewhere, including items such as unusual grading, drainage structures, retaining walls, fence, railings, and accessory structures.)

_____
_____
_____

Continued on page 77

LANDSCAPING, PLANTING, AND FINISH GRADING:

Topsoil _____ " thick: ☐ front yard; ☐ side yards;

   ☐ rear yard to _____ feet behind main building.

Lawns *(seeded, sodded, or sprigged)*: ☐ front yard _; ☐ side yards _; ☐ rear yard _

Planting: ☐ as specified and shown on drawings; ☐ as follows:

_____Shade trees, deciduous, _____ "caliper.	
_____Low flowing trees, deciduous,	_____' to _____'
_____High-growing shrubs, deciduous,	_____' to _____'
_____Medium-growing shrubs, deciduous,	_____' to _____'
_____Low-growing shrubs, deciduous,	_____' to _____'
_____Evergreen trees,	_____' to _____', B & B.
_____Evergreen shrubs,	_____' to _____', B & B.
_____Vines, 2-year _____	

_____

_____

Identification. — This exhibit shall be identified by the signature of the builder, or sponsor, and/or the proposed mortgagor if the latter is known at the time of application.

Date_____   Signature _____

                          Signature _____

FHA Form 2005
VA Form 26-1852

CERTIFICATE OF INSURANCE

Name and Address of Party to
Whom this Certificate is Issued

Name and Address of Insured

INSURANCE
IN FORCE

TYPE OF INSURANCE AND HAZARDS	POLICY FORMS	LIMITS OF LIABILITY	POLICY NUMBER	EXPIRATION DATE
Workmen's Compensation		STATUTORY*		
Employers' Liability	STANDARD	$ PER ACCIDENT (Employer's Liability only) *Applies only in following state(s):		

Automobile Liability		Bodily Injury Each	Property Damage		
☐ OWNED ONLY	☐ BASIC	$ PERSON			
☐ NON-OWNED ONLY	☐ COMPRE-HENSIVE	$. ACCIDENT	$		
☐ HIRED ONLY	☐ GARAGE	$ OCCURRENCE	$		
		Bodily Inj. and Prop. Dam. (Single Limit)			
☐ OWNED, NON-OWNED AND HIRED	☐	$ EACH ACCIDENT			
		$ EACH OCCURRENCE			

General Liability		Bodily Injury	Property Damage	
☐ PREMISES – O.L.&T.	☐ SCHEDULE	$ EACH PERSON		
☐ OPERATIONS – M.&C.		$ EACH ACCIDENT	$	
☐ ELEVATOR	☐ COMPRE-HENSIVE	$ EACH OCCURRENCE	$	
☐ PRODUCTS/ COMPLETED OPERATIONS		$ AGGREG. PROD. COMP. OPTNS.	$	
☐ PROTECTIVE (Independent Contractors)	☐ SPECIAL MULTI-PERIL	AGGREGATE OPERATIONS	$	
☐ Endorsed to cover contract between insured and	☐	AGGREGATE PROTECTIVE	$	
		AGGREGATE CONTRACTUAL	$	
_____		Bodily Inj. and Prop. Dam. (Single Limit)		
_____		$ EACH ACCIDENT		
_____		$ EACH OCCURRENCE		
date_____		$ AGGREGATE		

Continued on page 79

The policies identified above by number are in force on the date indicated below. With respect to a number entered under policy number, the type of insurance shown at its left is in force, but only with respect to such of the hazards, and under such policy forms, for which an "X" is entered, subject, however, to all the terms of the policy having reference thereto. The limits of liability for such insurance are only as shown above. This Certificate of Insurance neither affirmatively nor negatively amends, extends, nor alters the coverage afforded by the policy or policies numbered in this Certificate.

In the event of reduction of coverage or cancellation of said policies, the_____ Company will make all reasonable effort to send notice of such reduction or cancellation to the certificate holder at the address shown above.

THIS CERTIFICATE IS ISSUED AS A MATTER OF INFORMATION ONLY AND CONFERS NO RIGHTS UPON THE CERTIFICATE HOLDER.

Date_____, 19____ By _____
                                    Authorized Representative

U454-16
(8-81)

FIXED PRICE CONTRACT

Contractor: _____

Owner: _____ Date: _____

Owner is or shall become fee-simple owner of a structure known or described as:

_____

Contractor hereby agrees to renovate the structure described above according to the plans drawn by _____

and the specifications herein attached.

Owner shall pay Contractor for the renovation of said structure $ _____ .

Prior to commencement hereunder, owner shall secure financing for the renovation of said structure in the amount of $ _____ which loan shall be disbursed from time-to-time as renovation progresses, subject to a holdback of no more than 10 percent. Owner hereby authorizes Contractor to submit a request for draws in the name of the Owner from the savings and loan, or similar institution, up to the completed percentage of renovation and to accept said draws in partial payment thereof.

Contractor shall commence renovation as soon as feasible after closing, and shall pursue work to a scheduled completion on or before seven (7) months from commencement, except if such completion shall be delayed by unusually unfavorable weather, strikes, natural disasters, unavailability of labor or materials, or changes in the plans and specifications.

Contractor shall renovate the residence in substantial compliance with the plans and specifications and in a good workmanlike manner, and shall meet all building code requirements. Contractor shall not be responsible for failure of materials or equipment that are not Contractor's fault. Except as herein set out, Contractor shall make no representations or warranties with respect to the work to be done hereunder.

Owner shall not occupy the residence and Contractor shall hold the keys until all work has been completed and all monies due Contractor hereunder have been paid.

Owner shall not make any changes to the plans and specifications until such changes shall be evidenced in writing; the costs, if any, of such changes shall be set out; and any additional costs thereof shall be paid in advance of the work being accomplished.

Contractor shall not be obligated to continue work hereunder in the event Owner shall breach any term or condition hereof, or if for any reason construction draws shall cease to be advanced upon proper request.

Any additional or special stipulations attached hereto and signed by the parties shall be and are made a part hereof.

Contractor _____ (seal)

Owner: _____ (seal)

_____ (seal)

FIXED FEE CONTRACT

Contractor: _____

Owner: _____ Date: _____

Owner is or shall become fee-simple owner of a structure known or described as:

_____ .

Contractor hereby agrees to renovate the structure described above according to the plans and specifications identified as Exhibit A. Plans and specifications drawn on _____ by _____ .

Owner shall pay Contractor for the renovation of said structure, cost of construction, and a fee of $ _____ . Cost of construction is estimated in Exhibit B. Each item in Exhibit B is an estimate and is not to be construed as an exact cost.

Owner shall secure or has secured financing for the renovation of said structure in the amount of $ _____ , which shall be disbursed by a savings and loan or bank from time-to-time as construction progresses, subject to a holdback of no more than 10 percent. Owner hereby authorizes Contractor to submit a request for draws, in the name of the Owner under such loan, up to the completed percentage of construction and to accept said draws in partial payment hereof. In addition, it is understood that the Contractor's fee shall be paid in installments by the savings and loan or bank at the time of, and as a part of, each construction draw as a percentage of completion, so that the entire fee shall be paid at or before the final construction draw.

Contractor shall commence work as soon as feasible after closing of the construction loan and shall pursue work to a scheduled completion on or before seven (7) months from commencement, except if such completion shall be delayed by unusually unfavorable weather, strikes, natural disasters, unavailability of labor or materials, or changes in the plans or specifications.

Contractor shall renovate the residence in substantial compliance with the plans and specifications and in a good and workmanlike manner, and shall meet all building codes. Contractor shall not be responsible for failure of materials or equipment not Contractor's fault. Except as herein set out, Contractor shall make no representations or warranties with respect to the work to be done hereunder.

Owner shall not occupy the residence and Contractor shall hold the keys until all work has been completed and all monies due Contractor hereunder shall have been paid.

Owner shall not make changes to the plans or specifications until such changes shall be evidenced in writing; the costs, if any, of such changes shall be set out; and the construction lender and Contractor shall have approved such changes. Any additional costs thereof shall be paid in advance, or payment guaranteed in advance of the work being accomplished.

Contractor shall not be obligated to continue work hereunder in the event Owner shall breach any term or condition hereof, or if for any reason the construction lender shall cease making advances under the construction loan upon proper request thereof.

Any additional or special stipulations attached hereto and signed by the parties shall be and are made a part hereof.

Contractor: _____ (seal)

Owner: _____ (seal)

_____ (seal)

SUBCONTRACTOR'S INVOICE

Request Number: _____

To: _____   Contractor: _____
_____   _____
_____   _____

Date: _____   Contract number: _____

Change order number: _____

Workmens Comp. Ins. Co.: _____

Job Name	Job No.	Description of Work	Amount	

Work Completed in Accordance   Total: _____
with Contract:

                                       Less retainage: _____

_____
          (Contractor)   _____

                                       Net amount due: _____

SAMPLE SPECIFICATIONS

Site Work

Subterranean termite control. Subterranean termite control shall be performed by a licensed pest-control operator for wood-destroying organisms, licensed by the state, who has been engaged in the business of pest control for a period of not less than 5 years.

Application Technique. Treatment shall not be made when the soil is excessively wet, to avoid surface flow of the toxicant from the application site. Adequate precautions shall be taken to prevent disturbance of the treatment, and human or animal contact with the treated soil.

Guarantee. Upon completion of the soil treatment, and as a condition for its final acceptance, the Contractor shall furnish to the Owner a written guarantee providing:

A. that the chemical, having at least required concentration, and the rate and method of application, applies in every respect with the standards contained herein and;
B. that the Contractor guarantees the effectiveness of the soil-treatment against termite infestation for a period of not less than 10 years from date of treatment. Any evidence of reinfestation within the guarantee period will require treatment without additional expense to the Owner. The guarantee shall be in a form acceptable to the architect and shall be drawn in favor of the Owner, successor, or assignee.

Concrete

Requirements of the contractor documents apply to all work in this division.

Concrete work. The work included in this division shall consist of the furnishing, placing, and reinforcing of all concrete and cement work necessary to erect this work such as all footings, tunnels, u-block beam lintels, pedestals, piers, floor slabs, cement floor finishes, exterior stoops, trenches and such other work shown and specified. Footings shall be constructed on level beds and shall be carried below the lowest established frost line. No footings shall be constructed on frozen soil. On sloping ground, all footings shall be carried to a sufficient depth to prevent undermining by erosion.

Minimum compressive strength. Concrete shall have a minimum compressive-strength at twenty-eight (28) days of at least the design strength of the particular use, but not less than 3,000 pounds per square inch.

Masonry

Masonry installation. All masonry shall be laid strength-level plumb and true per Structural Clay Products Institution's latest edition.

Mortar. Natural shall conform to ASTM C-91 for Type M masonry cement.

Brick. All brick below grade, not exposed to view, shall be new, whole, hard, burned, common brick, Grace MW.

Joint treatment. Tool joints.

Carpentry

The requirements of the contract documents apply to all work in this division.

Scope of work. Furnish and install all carpentry items and labor hereinafter noted and reasonably intended on the plans such as joists, sills, girders, plates, studs, bracing, sheathing and subflooring, decking, stripping, blocking, etc., and finish carpentry.

Measurements. The Contractor shall obtain, at the building, all measurements checked with details and be responsible for same. He or she shall establish the finished lines and coordinate the work of the various trades.

Quality of workmanship. All work that is to be performed under these specifications shall be done by mechanics and artisans skilled in their respective trades in order to produce first-class construction and installation of the work. All framing shall be set level, plumb, set to align, and well braced into place. (See drawings for sizes.)

Framing lumber. Framing, grounds, blocking, etc., shall be southern yellow pine, no. 2, 2-inch dimension with an "F" of 1,200 p.s.i.

Standards and specifications. All standards and specifications mentioned in this section refer to the latest editions unless otherwise stated and shall be considered a part of this specification.

National design specification for stress grade lumber and its fastenings. All sections make reference to this specification for all lumber uses and fastenings.

Materials.
   Wall bracing: Let-in 1 X 4 or approved metal braces at all corners.
   Exposed framing: Select structural no. 2 yellow pine, treated.
   Subfloors: Store: 1 X 6 SYP laid diagonally. Apts: Existing. Lofts: ¾ T & G Plywood.
   Roof sheathing: ½-inch plywood exterior grade or 1 X 6 kiln dried sheathing boards.

Wall sheathing: ½-inch rigid urethane foam, R-4, foil-faced both sides.

Exterior decking: 2 X 6, no. 2 yellow pine, treated.

Railings at exterior decks: 2 X 6, top cap; 4 X 4 intermediate posts: 2 X 2 balusters with 2 X 4 bottom rail.

Construction.

Joists: Double joists for all headers and trimmers and under all partitions running parallel to the joists.

Blocking: For each runner joist, install solid block or 1 X 3 cross bridging. Two rows for stands over 12 feet and three rows for stands over 15 feet.

Blocking: Required 24 inches on-center vertically in walls to receive vertical siding.

Nails: Shall be stainless steel hot-dipped galvanized or aluminum for all exposed framing and siding. Nailing schedule as per approved edition of the Uniform Building Code.

Finish carpentry materials.

Exterior siding: 1 X 6 masonite lap siding with 4½-inch exposure.

Wood louvers: Build in wood louvers where shown, in pine as specified.

Screening: Provide exterior aluminum bird screen on louvers and continuous strip of soffit.

Soffits and ceilings: Shall be ⅜-inch A/C plywood, painted.

Wood fascia and trim: Unless otherwise noted, exterior mill work will be of "B" and better grade kiln dried yellow pine, clear and free from knots.

Interior door and window trim and base: Shall be white pine, painted.

Joints: Miter all joints.

Case work: By Owner.

Stairs: Apt. 2 — triple 2 X 12 stringers with ¾-inch SYP riser and 1¼-inch heartpine treads.

Ladders: Apt. 1 and 2 (to lofts) — 2 X 8 fir stringers with 1¼-inch treads rabbeted into stringer.

Wainscot: Material by Owner. Install as indicated in drawings.

Moisture Protection

Roofing and related work.

Built-up roofing: 5 ply, 20-year bondable, commenced washed opaque gravel topping.

Rigid Insulation: Shall be square edged, coated top surface, noncombustible fiberboard, 2' X 4' with "C" value of 0.12, shall be fesco board. Contractor's option; rigid fiberglass or rigid fiberboard with minimum thickness of ½ inch and equal "C" value will be considered equal.

Gravel Stops and Flashing: 26 gauge, hot-dipped galvanized iron, painted.

Installation. All roofing or related work shall be installed as per the manufacturer's recommendations for a watertight installation including projections through the roof. Installation shall be only by roofing mechanics experienced in the roofing type to be installed.

Metal roofing. Metal roofing shall be 5-V crimp galvanized roofing. Provide ridge cap and nails.

Cleaning. Clean all tar from exposed surfaces.

Guarantee. Roofer shall furnish a 5-year written guarantee covering all defects connected with the installation of the roof.

Dampproofing and waterproofing through wall flashing. Provide flashing around all openings and wall over door and window heads and under sills plus any incidental flashing necessary to make the building watertight.

Caulking. Natural color by Tremco in strict accordance with the manufacturer's recommendations.

Roof accessories.

Roof vents: Painted galvanized iron.

Insulation: Building paper shall be 15 pounds asphalt saturated felt.

Wall insulation: Shall be fiberglass wool batts, thickness to fill full width between studs, R-13.

Floor insulation: Shall be fiberglass wool batts, thickness to fill full width between joists, R-19.

Roof insulation: Rigid at built-up roof, 6-inch fiberglass batts at rafters.

Doors, Windows and Glass

Requirements of the Contract Documents apply to all work in this Division.

Finish Hardware. Quality of hardware will be Builder's Hardware manufactured by Kwikset or equal and shall be approved by the architect prior to use.

Wood doors.

Entry doors: Shall be solid core, 1¾-inch thick, 3' X 6'8".

Bi-folding doors: 1⅜-inch wood paneled.

Interior doors: Solid wood paneled 1⅜-inches thick.

Windows. Existing windows shall be reworked to original condition. Care shall be taken to salvage existing glass for reuse.

Storefront. Sizes on drawings are approximate. Actual sizes shall be determined by measuring in the field. Glazier shall check all field dimensions prior to fabrication and delivery.

Sheet glass. Shall be new and clean; sizes as noted or required by the Uniform Building Code.

Insulating glass. ½-inch thick, clear.

Tempered insulating glass. ½-inch clear; use at entrances, glass filled doors and storefront.

Glazing compound. Shall be permanently elastic.

Cleaning. Clean all glass surfaces after installation.

Weatherstripping. Provide bronze interlocking type weatherstripping at head and jamb of all exterior doors.

Window Weatherstripping. Shall be integral factory installed.

Threshold. Provide oak saddle type thresholds at all exterior doors.

Finish hardware.
   Schedule: Hardware schedule shall be submitted to the architect for approval.
   Lock sets and door pulls: Kwikset or equal.

Finishes

Gypsum Wallboard. Wallboard shall be ½-inch gypsum sheetrock or ⅝-inch fire rated sheetrock as noted on the plans.

Edging. Provide metal edging at exposed edges and external corners.

Nailing. Deep set nails or use screws to prevent popping. Compound each nailing point and sand smooth.

Joint treatment. Taping compound joints per manufacturer's recommendations; sand after each application of joint compound.

Holes. All holes cut for switches, receptacles, light fixtures, and plumbing pipes are to be made with drywall cutting tool so that all cover plates completely conceal all rough edges.

Finish. Painted flat by Owner.

Painting. By Owner.

Carpeting. By Owner.

Wood floors. Repair hardwood floors and prepare for refinishing by Owner.

Specialties

Toilet and Bath Accessories. By Owner.

Foundation vents. Aluminum screen on treated 1 X 2 frame nailed to interior face of foundation wall.

Soffit screen vent. Continuous aluminum insect screen.

Equipment.
Prefinished cabinet work and appliances by Owner.

Mechanical

Heating and air-conditioning. Installation as per applicable codes and enforced with standards of the American Society of Heating, Refrigeration and Air-Conditioning Engineers (ASHRAE).

Scope of Services. The Contractor for work provided by this section shall furnish all labor equipment, appliances, etc., in connection with the complete installation, ready for use, of the items specified herein in strict accordance with the specifications and general conditions and the heating and air-conditioning work indicated on drawings. The Contractor shall coordinate work with the other trades to avoid interference. All work and related items necessary to complete the work, whether shown on the drawings or specified or both, are part of this contract.

Installation. As per applicable codes and in accordance with standards at the American Society of Heating, Refrigeration and Air-Conditioning Engineers.

Flashing. Provide flashing and counterflashing as necessary for a watertight job. Coordinate with roofing contractor where pipes and ducts pass through walls or roof.

Duct work. Fabricated or galvanized sheetmetal, 24 gauge minimum.

Duct insulation. Provide 1-inch or 1½-inch fiberglass on galvanized metal ducts.

Vertical return ducts. Shall be ½-inch acoustic-lined.

Heating and cooling units. Apartments number 1 and 2; one each, 1½-ton heat pump and air-handler by General Electric.

Store. One 3-ton heat pump and air-handler by General Electric.

Work included. The work specified under this section of the specifications includes but is not limited to the following:

  a. Electric heat pump, air-handling and condensing units for each conditioned space.
  b. Supply exhaust and return airduct work.
  c. Exhaust fans for bathrooms.
  d. Grilles and registers.
  e. Drain and refrigeration piping.
  f. Insulation.
  g. Controls.
  h. All other accessories and incidental items not itemized above but specified herinafter in this section of work.
  i. Provisions for all contingencies, and supply of all labor, materials, temporary electrical service, scaffolding, fixtures, tools, transportation, etc., necessary for proper installation of all work described in this section of the specifications and indicated on the drawings.

Guarantee. The Contractor shall guarantee all materials, equipment, and workmanship for a period of 12 months after the date of final acceptance of the building by the architect and Owner. All guarantee failures shall be corrected or replaced by the Contractor as soon as possible after notification of such failure. Compressors shall be guaranteed for 5 years.

Refrigerant piping. Type ACR dioxidized and sealed refrigerant copper tubing with wrought copper fittings. It shall conform to Federal Specifications WW-T-799 and ASTM B-83-33 and shall be free from scale and dirt. Precharged tubing also factory.

Drain-pan piping. Condensate lines shall be PVC.

Duct work. Galvanized iron or steel sheets, conforming to latest edition of the ASHRAE guide in every respect, including duct weight seams, joints, construction gauges, reinforcing and assembly. Mount with heavy straphangers bent at least 2 inches under bottom edges of the ducts. Sheet metal screws shall be stainless steel, cadmium plated or zinc plated. Any duct work that vibrates, buckles, wraps, sags, rumbles, or is not airtight for the service required, shall be corrected or replaced at the engineer's discretion. Air-turning veins of an approved type shall be provided in all square or short-rating elbows and where indicated on the drawings and details.

Insulation. No covering shall be applied until the work has been thoroughly cleaned and tested for tightness. The covering shall be applied in an approved manner and stripped in accordance with manufacturer's guide specifications and in no case shall be covered up or furred-in until inspected by the architect. All coverings shall be done by an approved insulation contractor qualified in this line of work. All coverings shall present a neat, smooth and finished appearance and shall be of fiberous glass unless otherwise specified.

Liquid refrigerant lines. No insulation required.

Suction refrigerant lines. Factory insulated or ¾-inch Armstrong foam plastic flexible insulation, Armorflex 22.

Cleanup. This Contractor shall keep the premises free of debris and unusable materials resulting from work, and as work progresses, or upon request, the General Contractor shall remove such debris and materials from the Owner's property and leave all floors broom-clean in areas affected by the work. All fixtures to be cleaned to the satisfaction of the architect and the Owner.

Control system. Controls shall be provided for systems where indicated on the drawings.

Plumbing

Scope of work. The Contractor for work covered by this section shall furnish all labor, materials, equipment, appliances, etc., in connection with the complete installation, ready for use, of the items specified herein in strict accordance with this section of the specifications and the general conditions in the plumbing work as indicated on the drawings. The Contractor shall coordinate the work with the other trades to avoid interference. All work and related items necessary to complete the work, whether shown on the drawings or specified or both are a part of this contract.

Work included. The work specified under this section of the specifications includes, but is not limited to, the following:

1. The installation of proper water services within the building.
2. Furnish and install all plumbing fixtures where shown on the drawings.
3. The installation of the soil waste vent and drain piping, connections to sanitary sewer system.
4. Furnishing complete installation of the domestic hot water heaters where shown on the drawings.
5. The complete installation of all hot and cold water piping.

Rules and regulations.

1. All work shall be in accordance with rules and regulations of the state applicable, local rules and regulations, and of any authorities having jurisdiction insofar as such regulations apply to the work or material provided under this contract.
2. The Contractor shall make all necessary arrangements and pay for all necessary fees, charges, and permits required for the complete installation of the work.

Materials. Materials shall conform to the designated standards of the American Standards Association (ASA), American Water Works Association (AWWA), Commercial Standards (CS), and Cast-Iron Soil Pipe Institute (CISPI).

Protection. Protect all work from damage and properly close all pipes with test plugs, screw caps, etc., to prevent foreign matter from entering the pipes during construction.

Flashings. For gable or sloping roofs, flashing shall be standard 2½-pound all lead flashing unit with lead band at the top. Lead shall be crimped watertight around pipe in a form flashing under metal roof and built-up roof.

Domestic hot water heater. Heater shall be furnished and installed by the plumbing contractor for the living unit. Heaters are to be UL approved, quick recovery, and glass lined.

Cutting and patching. In areas where it is necessary to cut concrete floors, walls, and ceilings to install soil waste vent or hot and cold water piping, the plumbing contractor shall do the cutting and patching. Piping shall be installed without critical damage to structural members. Holes drilled shall be at the center line of the structural member.

Plumbing fixtures.

1. Reuse existing clawfoot tub, new fittings.
2. New water closet and tank set.

3. Install Owner's pedestal lavatory, new fittings.
4. Furnish new stainless steel kitchen sink, twin compartment.
5. Furnish one 40-gallon water heater with pan.
6. Connect Owner's garbage disposal.
7. Connect Owner's dishwasher.
8. Furnish hookup for ice maker.
9. Reuse existing fixtures in bathrooms.
10. Install one wall-mounted lavatory.
11. Install one 30-gallon water heater.
12. Install new fittings for lavatory and tank sets.

Acceptance. All work furnished under this section of the specifications shall be thoroughly cleaned and ready for use of the Owner. Upon completion of the entire system covered by these specifications, a certificate of approval from the different city departments that have jurisdiction shall be obtained and then delivered to the Owner.

Guarantee. The Contractor shall guarantee and service all workmanship and materials, and shall repair or replace, at no additional cost, any part thereof which may become defective within the period of 12 months after the date of final acceptance. Ordinary wear and tear accepted.

Cleanup. This Contractor shall keep the premises free from debris and unusable materials resulting from his work and as work progresses, or upon request from the General Contractor shall remove such debris and materials from the Owner's property and leave all floors broom-clean in areas affected by his work.

Electrical

Scope of Work. The Contractor for this section shall provide all labor, materials, equipment, and services necessary for, and reasonably incidental to, the completion of all work shown on the drawings and detail sheets as herein specified.
Feeders, panels boards, circuit wiring, outlet, and connections complete to meter box as required.
Connection of equipment as specified.
Lighting fixtures complete.
TV outlet box.
Telephone outlet boxes.

Regulations. The installation of the electrical wiring shall conform with the National Electrical Codes, the local code, and the requirements of the local power company. All materials shall be new and shall be listed by Underwriters Laboratory, Inc., as conforming to its standards in every case for which such a standard has been established for the particular material in question. The Contractor shall effectively protect, at his or her expense, the electrical installation from injury during the construction period, all openings into any part of the conduit system, as well as associated fixtures, equipment, etc., but

before and after being set in place must be securely covered or otherwise protected to prevent obstruction of the tools and materials by grit or any other foreign matter. The Contractor will be held responsible for all damage so done until the work is fully and finally accepted. Conduit ends shall be covered with capped bushings.

Certificate of inspection. All interior electrical work is to be inspected and approved by the local electrical inspector before the system is energized. Duplicate certificates of this approval shall be delivered to the Owner. All fees for the above and for any other inspection and approval service required shall be borne by the Contractor.

Character of materials and equipment. All materials and equipment, except here and otherwise specified, shall be new and conform with standards specified herein. Equipment is herein defined to include conduits, cable, wiring, materials and devices, panel boards, etc. All equipment offered under these specifications shall be limited to products produced and recommended for service ratings in accordance with manufacturer's catalogue, engineering data, or other comprehensive literature that may be available to the public. Equipment shall be installed in strict accordance with the manufacturer's instructions for type capacity and suitability of each piece of equipment used. This Contractor shall obtain instructions which shall be considered a part of these specifications.

Field Measurements. The Contractor shall take all field measurements necessary for this work and shall assume responsibility for their accuracy.

Drawings and specifications. The drawings are intended to show the general arrangement of outlets. Door swings shall be checked for final arrangement. The Contractor shall check all structural and mechanical plans and specifications so that he or she may coordinate work with these trades. All outlets shall be located uniformly with respective beams, partitions, ducts, openings, etc., and the general location shall be checked before installing. Should there be any interference between the electrical outlets and other trades, the Contractor shall notify the Owner so that proper location may be decided upon. No outlets shall be installed in inaccessible places.

Permits. The Electrical Contractor shall obtain all permits required for the work, including the cost of same in the estimate.

TV system. The Contractor shall install an outlet box in each apartment. The cable to the outlet is to be furnished and installed by the Owner.

Receptacles and switches.
Receptacles: General receptacles shall be Arrow-Hart no. 5242 or Leviton no. 5014.
Receptacles for ranges: Leviton no. 5050.

Bathroom ground fault receptacles: Square D No. GFR-115, 15 amp capacity.

Weatherproof Receptacles: to be ground fault receptacles.

Switches: Boxes of a class to satisfy the conditions for each outlet shall be used in concealed work. Boxes shall be installed in a rigid and satisfactory manner. Switches shall be Arrow-Hart no. 1101 or Leviton no. 5501.

Connection to mechanical equipment. The Contractor is cautioned to note carefully other sections of these specifications describing equipment to be furnished under these sections, in order that he or she may fully understand the wiring requirements. All power wiring and switches for apartment air-conditioning units, exhaust fans and water heaters shall be furnished and installed by the Electrical Contractor. Exposed connections to water heaters shall be made with junction boxes on the wall.

Telephone outlets. The Contractor shall make all necessary arrangements with the telephone company for the installation of telephone cables and terminals and coordinate the work to insure the installation at the proper time.

Lighting fixtures. The Contractor shall furnish and install lighting fixtures as scheduled on the drawings. All fixtures shall bear the Underwriters label.

Smoke detectors. The Contractor shall furnish and install smoke detectors.

Guarantee. The Contractor shall leave the entire electrical system, installed under this contract, in proper working order and shall, without charge, replace any working materials which develop defects, except ordinary wear and tear, within 12 months from the date of final inspection and acceptance.

Cleanup. This Contractor shall keep the premises free of debris and unusual materials resulting from the work, as work progresses, or upon request by the General Contractor, shall remove such debris and materials from the Owner's property and leave all floors broom-clean in areas affected by the work.

Service. Provide 200 amp main service. Wire heat pump high and low voltage. Provide wiring for heat pumps, air handlers, dishwasher, disposal, stove, water heater, kitchen circuit, lighting, and receptacle circuits as per plans.

Allowances. Total light fixture allowance $ _____ . Total equipment and appliances allowance $ _____ , which includes stove, refrigerator, range hood, and bath fan.

SAMPLE BLUEPRINTS

Knight Residence. Plans

(Courtesy, John M. Knight)

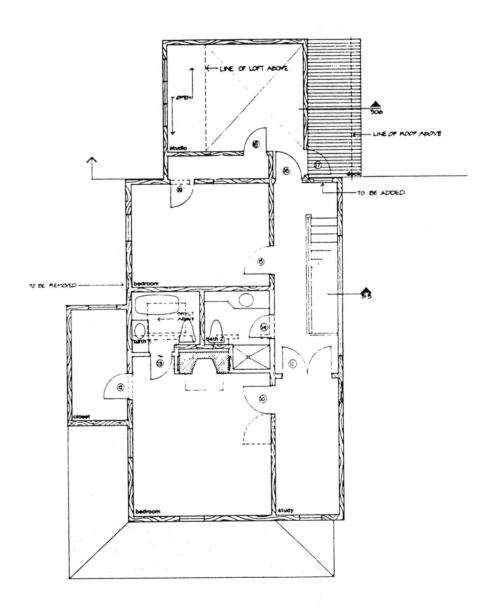

102 second level

DOOR SCHEDULE					
NO.	TYPE	R.O. W	H	HD.HT.	REMARKS
01					BY OWNER
02					
03					
04					
05					BY OWNER
06					
07					
08					BY OWNER
09					
10					
11					
12					
13					
14					BY OWNER
15					
16					
17					

WINDOW SCHEDULE					
NO.	TYPE	R.O. W	H	HD.HT.	REMARKS
01					BY OWNER
02					
03					
04					
05					
06					
07					BY OWNER
08					
09					
10					
11					
12					
13					BY OWNER
14					
15					
16					BY OWNER

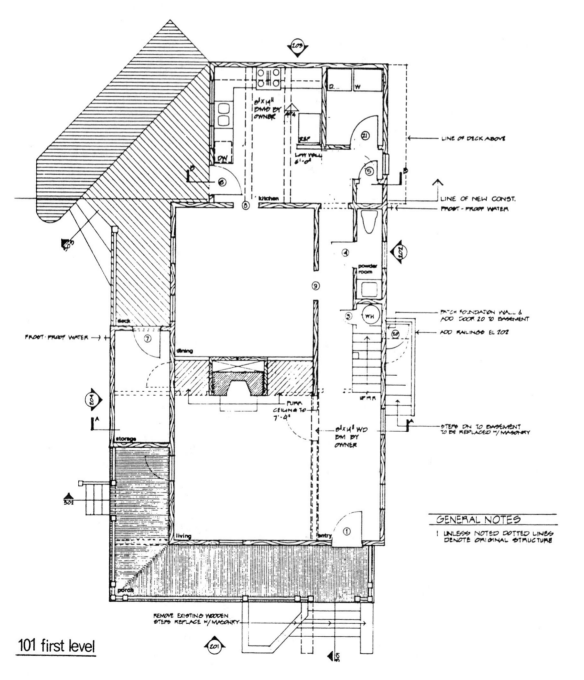

GENERAL NOTES

1 UNLESS NOTED DOTTED LINES
DENOTE ORIGINAL STRUCTURE

101 first level

Knight Residence. Elevations

2 north

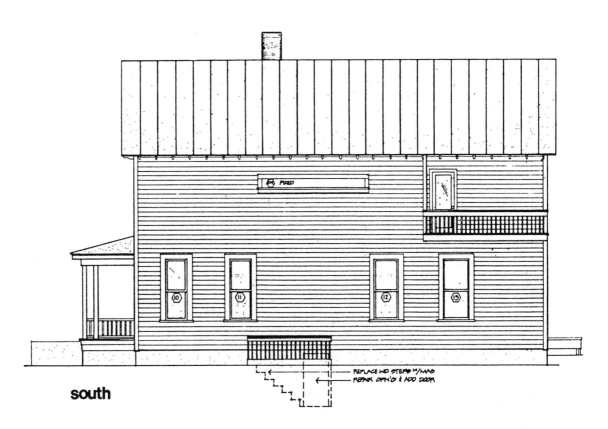

south

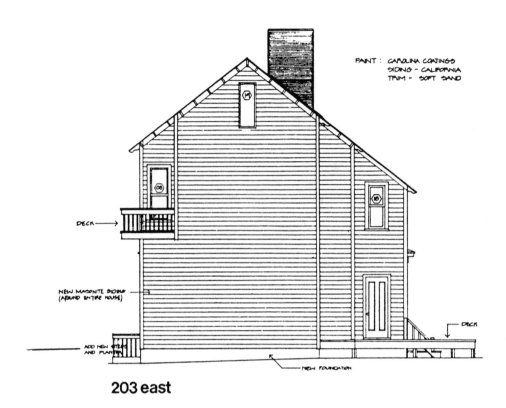

PAINT : CAROLINA COATINGS
SIDING - CALIFORNIA
TRIM - SOFT SAND

DECK →

NEW MASONITE SIDING
(AROUND ENTIRE HOUSE)

DECK

ADD NEW STEPS
AND PLANTERS

NEW FOUNDATION

203 east

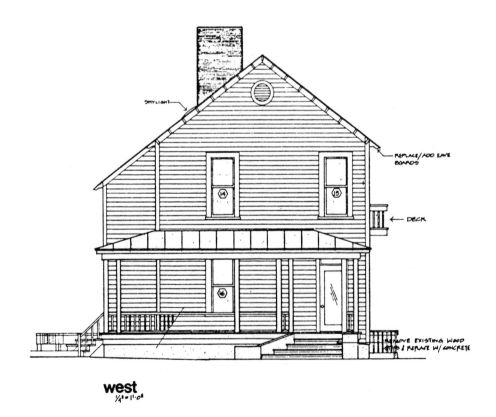

SKYLIGHT

REPLACE/ADD EAVE
BOARDS

← DECK

REMOVE EXISTING WOOD
STEPS & REPLACE W/ CONCRETE

west
1/4" = 1'-0"

Knight Residence. Details

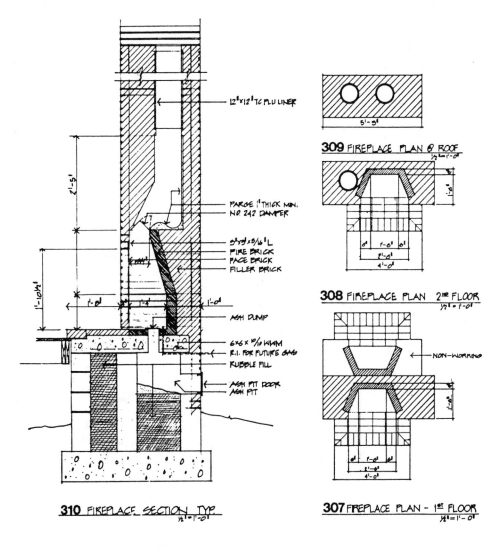

310 FIREPLACE SECTION TYP.

309 FIREPLACE PLAN @ ROOF

308 FIREPLACE PLAN 2ND FLOOR

307 FIREPLACE PLAN - 1ST FLOOR

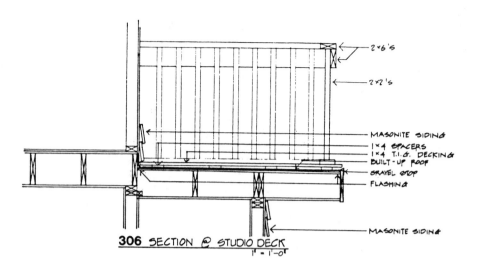

2×6's

2×2's

MASONITE SIDING
1×4 SPACERS
1×4 T.I.G. DECKING
BUILT-UP ROOF
GRAVEL STOP
FLASHING

MASONITE SIDING

306 SECTION @ STUDIO DECK
1" = 1'-0"

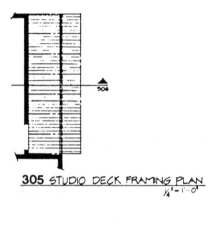

305 STUDIO DECK FRAMING PLAN
¼" = 1'-0"

306

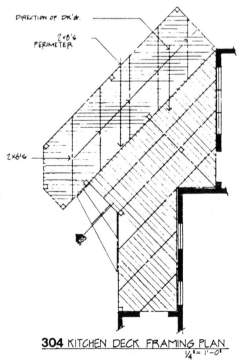

DIRECTION OF DK'G.

2×6'S
PERIMETER

2×6'S

304 KITCHEN DECK FRAMING PLAN
¼" = 1'-0"

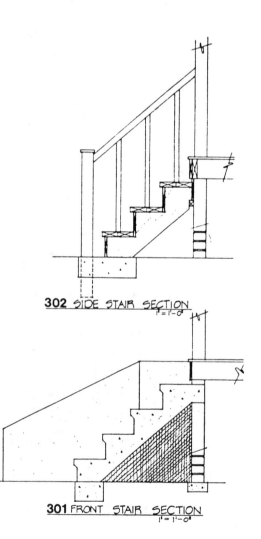

302 SIDE STAIR SECTION
1" = 1'-0"

301 FRONT STAIR SECTION
1" = 1'-0"

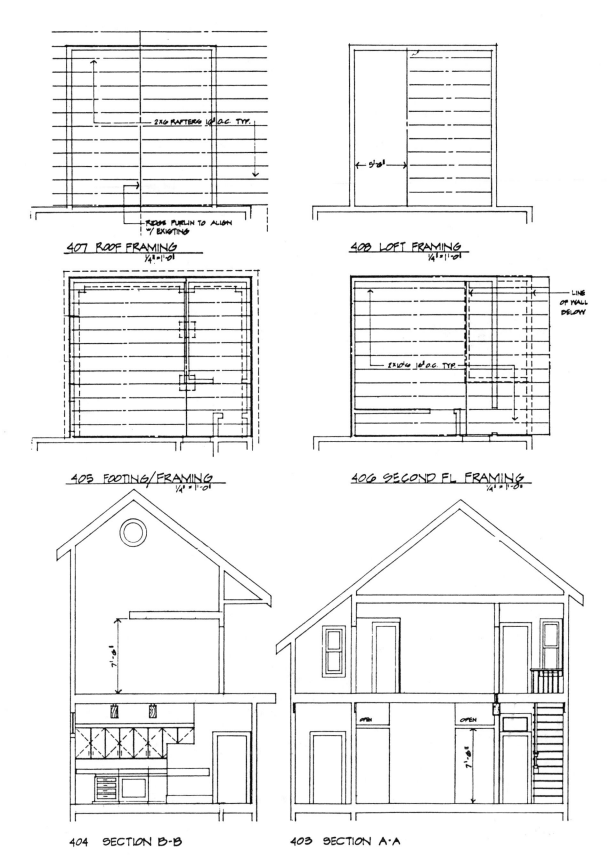

407 ROOF FRAMING
1/4" = 1'-0"

2X6 RAFTERS 16" O.C. TYP.

RIDGE PURLIN TO ALIGN
W/ EXISTING

408 LOFT FRAMING
1/4" = 1'-0"

5'-0"

405 FOOTING/FRAMING
1/4" = 1'-0"

406 SECOND FL FRAMING
1/4" = 1'-0"

2X10 16" O.C. TYP.

LINE
OF WALL
BELOW

404 SECTION B-B

7'-0"

403 SECTION A-A

OPEN   OPEN

7'-0"

Knight Residence. Site plan

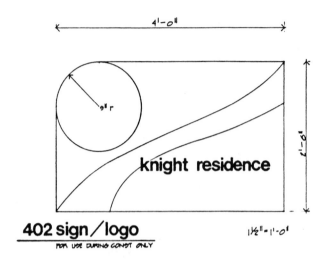

402 sign / logo
FOR USE DURING CONST ONLY

$1\frac{1}{2}" = 1'-0'$

W. EIGHTH ST.

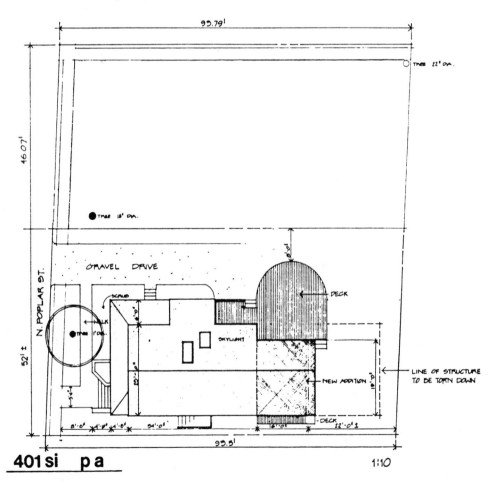

401 si   p a

1:10

Knight Residence. Electrical plan

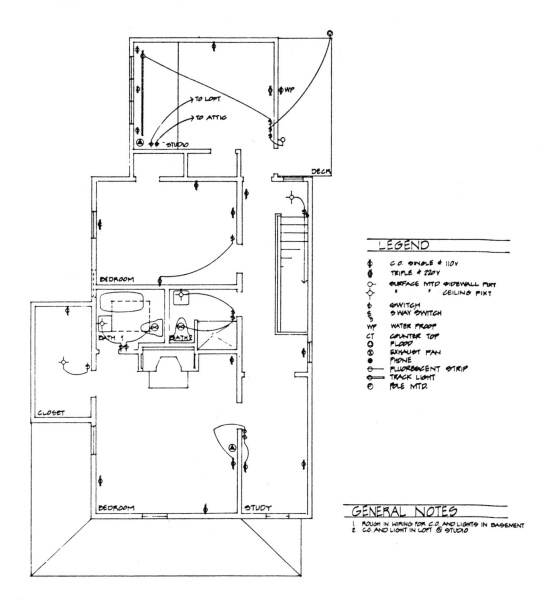

LEGEND

∅	C.O. SINGLE ∅ 110V
∅	TRIPLE ∅ 220V
○⟋	SURFACE MTD SIDEWALL FIXT
○⟋	" " CEILING FIXT
∮	SWITCH
∮₃	3 WAY SWITCH
WP	WATER PROOF
CT	COUNTER TOP
⊗	FLOOD
⊗	EXHAUST FAN
●	PHONE
⊖	FLUORESCENT STRIP
⊖	TRACK LIGHT
⊘	POLE MTD.

GENERAL NOTES

1. ROUGH IN WIRING FOR C.O. AND LIGHTS IN BASEMENT
2. C.O. AND LIGHT IN LOFT @ STUDIO

SECOND LEVEL

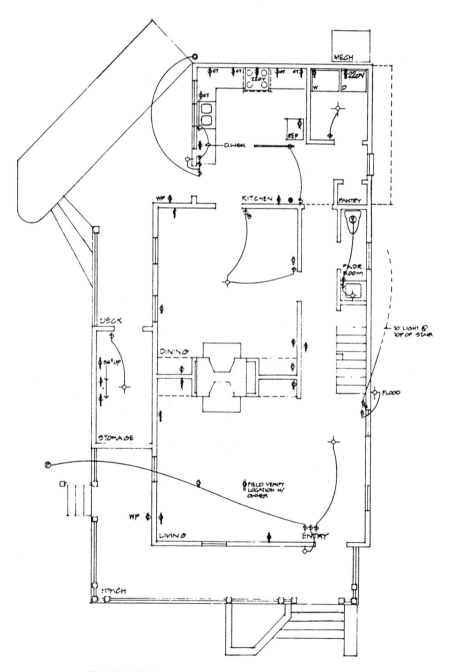

FIRST LEVEL

Reading the Plans

On the following pages are a set of plans, with each plan covering pages and drawn to serve a specific purpose.

For example, the plan on pages 100 and 101 is labeled "Foundation Plan" at the lower left corner. It shows all of the concrete work associated with this house, including the walls, piers, foundation for fireplace, and the slabs for the garage and the patio.

On pages 102 and 103 is the floor plan. Study yours, and ask yourself specific questions about living in a house that is built to your plan. Will you be happy with only a sliding glass door in the family room? Do you want to provide space for both a dining room, for formal dining, and a dinette, or would you prefer to make other use of one of those spaces? Do you want your garage doors opening to the rear of the house, or closer to the front entrance?

Look at the detail sheet on pages 104 and 105. It shows the second floor. Have you always wanted a fireplace in your master bedroom? It probably could be arranged — at extra cost. Will you be happy with the laundry up there (where most dirty clothes end up) or would you prefer it on the first floor?

Study the details on pages 106 and 107. Note the drawing on the left. It shows 3½ inches of insulation — the width of a common 2 x 4. Are you satisfied with that, or do you live in a cold climate where double that amount of insulation would pay for itself in lower fuel bills? Is the kitchen layout what you want, or are there points of it that will become irritations when it is used?

And finally, the outside elevations. Are you happy with its looks? Do you want that outside chimney, or would you prefer to see it inside, where its stored heat would be fed back into the home? Will you feel proud of this house when you drive up to it or when your friends do?

A thorough study of the plans should give you the feel of living in the house. You'll know where your TV set will be placed and your library of books. You'll have a place for the holiday decorations, the garden tools, the tools and equipment for your hobbies. Your furniture will fit in the spaces planned for it.

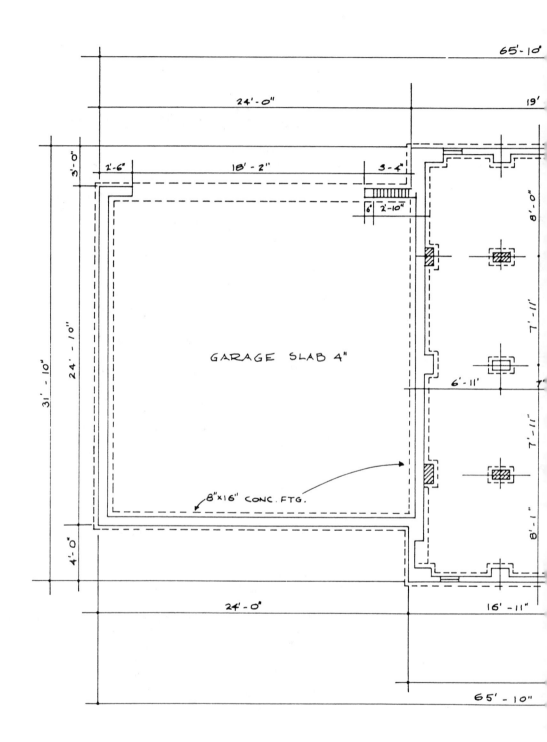

FOUNDATION PLAN

(Varies by design - shown is a house with a crawl space)

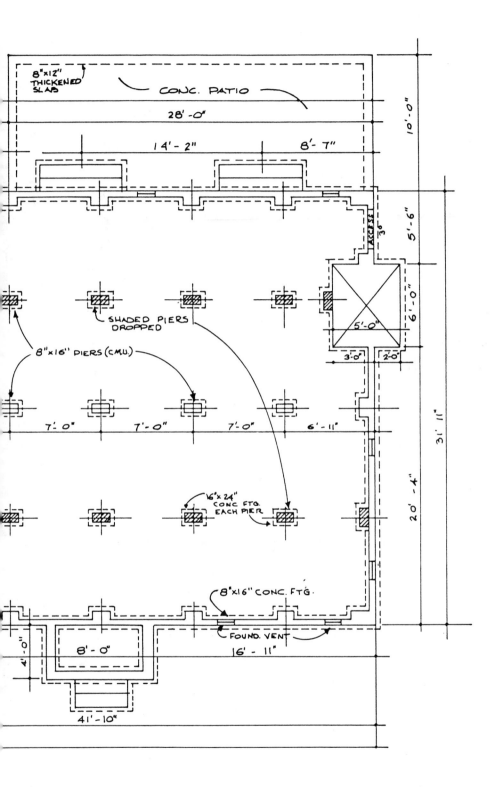

8"x12" THICKENED SLAB

CONC. PATIO

28'-0"

14'-2"

8'-7"

10'-0"

ACCESS

3'6"

5'-6"

6'-0"

5'-0"

SHADED PIERS DROPPED

8"x16" PIERS (C.M.U.)

3'-0"

2'-0"

7'-0"

7'-0"

7'-0"

6'-11"

31'-11"

16"x24" CONC. FTG. EACH PIER

8"x16" CONC. FTG.

20'-4"

FOUND. VENT

4'-0"

8'-0"

16'-11"

41'-10"

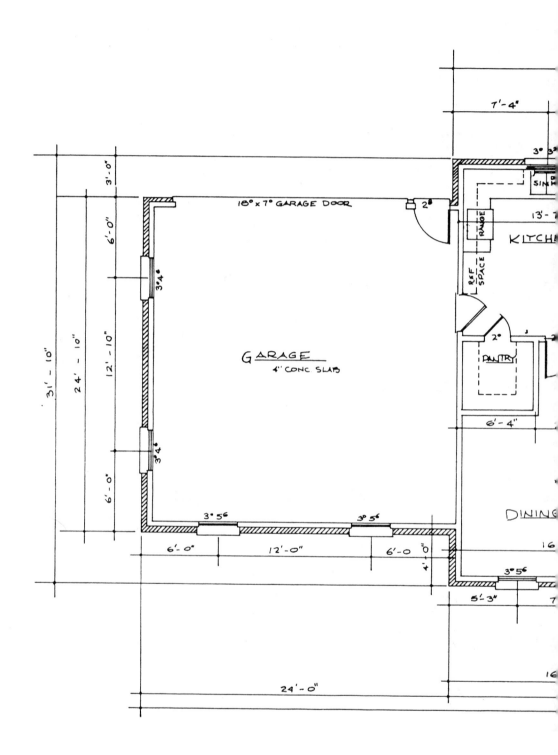

FLOOR PLAN

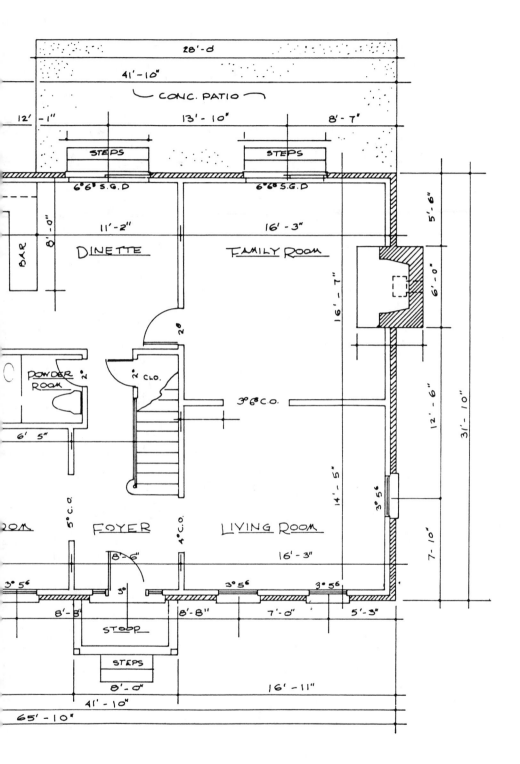

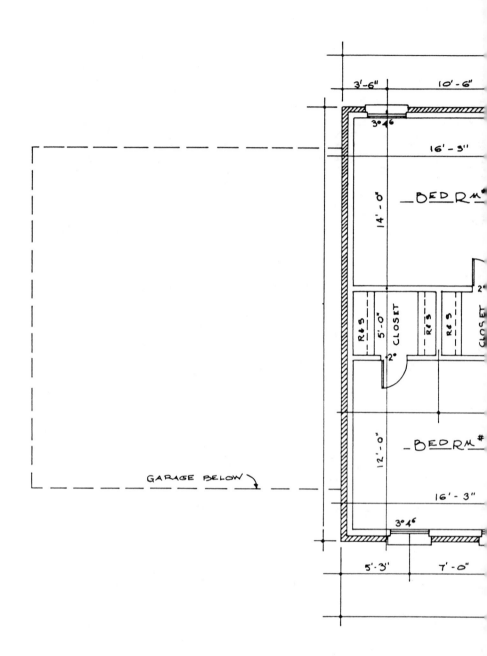

DETAIL SHEET

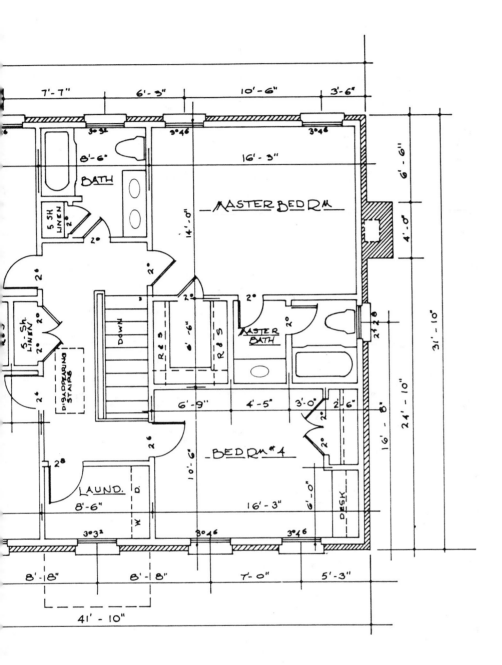

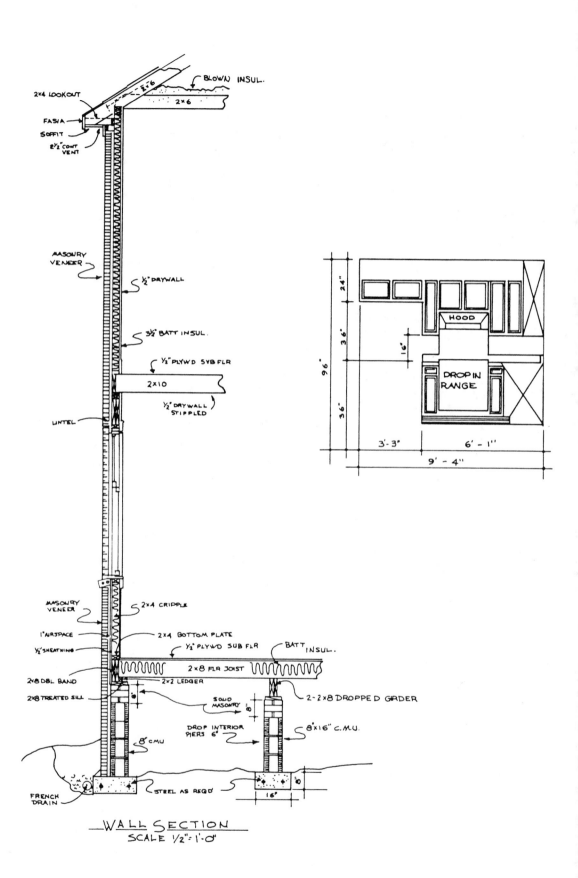

BLOWN INSUL.

2×4 LOOKOUT

2×6

FASIA

SOFFIT

2½" CONT VENT

MASONRY VENEER

½" DRYWALL

3½" BATT INSUL.

½" PLYWD SUB FLR

2×10

½" DRYWALL STIPPLED

LINTEL

MASONRY VENEER

2×4 CRIPPLE

1" AIRSPACE

½" SHEATHING

2×4 BOTTOM PLATE

½" PLYWD SUB FLR

BATT INSUL.

2×8 FLR JOIST

2×8 DBL BAND

2×2 LEDGER

2×8 TREATED SILL

SOLID MASONRY

2-2×8 DROPPED GIRDER

DROP INTERIOR PIERS 6"

8"×16" C.M.U.

8" CMU

FRENCH DRAIN

STEEL AS REQ'D

16"

WALL SECTION
SCALE ½"=1'-0"

24"

36"

96"

16"

HOOD

DROP IN RANGE

36"

3'-3"

6'-1"

9'-4"

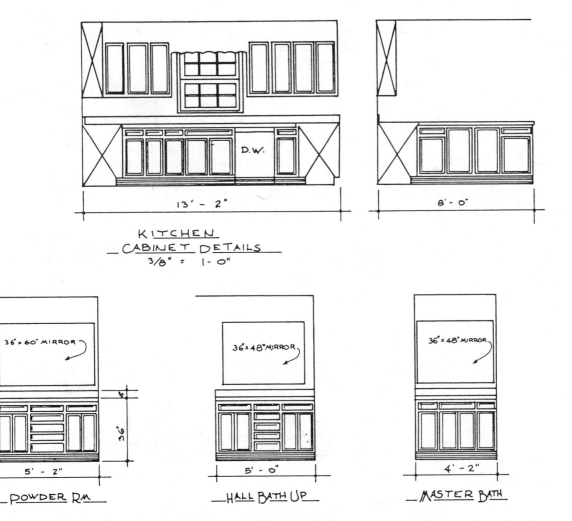

KITCHEN
CABINET DETAILS
3/8" = 1-0"

13' - 2"

8' - 0"

36" x 60" MIRROR

36" x 48" MIRROR

36" x 48" MIRROR

4"

36"

5' - 2"

5' - 0"

4' - 2"

POWDER RM

HALL BATH UP

MASTER BATH

RIGHT SIDE

REAR ELE

FRONT

OUTSIDE ELEVATIONS

LEFT SIDE

ELEVATION

Glossary

APPRAISED VALUE	An estimate of the value of property, such as a house.
APPRECIATES (appreciation)	Refers to the increase in value of a structure over a period of time.
BLUEPRINTS	A detailed plan of a structure.
BREAKER	Electrical circuit breaker. The modern version of the old-time fuse.
BRIDGE LOAN	A short-term loan to bridge the time between the purchase of one house and the sale of another.
BRICK VENEER	Brick used in lieu of siding.
BRIDGING	Small pieces of wood or metal used to brace floor joists.
BUILDING PLANS	See Blueprints.
BUILT UP ROOF	A type of roofing which consists of layers of felt building paper, asphalt, and stone.
CARPET UNDERLAYMENT	Either plywood or pressed wood (particle board) placed over the subfloor to make the floor more solid.
CAULKING	To fill cracks with a filler.
CERTIFICATE OF INSURANCE	Proof of insurance.
CHASE	A channel, as in a wall or ceiling, for something to lie in or pass through — electrical wiring, plumbing pipes, or vents.
CIRCUIT BREAKERS	Modern safety devices that prevent electrical overloads. They can be reset after reducing the load which caused them to trip.
CIRCUIT PANELS	See Panels.
CLEAR TITLE	A title (proof of ownership) of any property (land, auto, house) that is free of liens, mortgages, judgments, or any other encumbrance.
CLOSING	Specifically, a loan closing: completion of all legal documents necessary to procure a loan.
COLLATERAL	Something of monetary worth pledged to a lender for the purpose of securing a loan.
COLOR RUN	Materials produced using the same batch of dye, such as bricks, carpet, or paint. Subsequent batches may vary in color.
COMPRESSOR	Apparatus used to compress a gas called Freon for the purpose of cooling, or in the case of a heat pump for heating a structure.
CONTINGENCIES	Unforeseen, or chance, additional costs.
CONTRACT PRICE	A pre-agreed set price for a service or product.
COURSE	One row of bricks.

CRAWL SPACE	An area under a floor or roof in which there is insufficient height to stand.
DEED RESTRICTIONS	Encumbrances placed on a piece of real estate and filed at the county courthouse as a matter of record which restrict or prevent certain uses of that real estate.
DRAW	A disbursement of money that represents only a portion or percentage of the entire amount due the person.
DRIP CAP	A protective molding, usually metal, to divert water over an exterior surface.
DRY-IN	A stage in construction at which time the building is protected from rain and snow.
DRYWALL	Sheetrock.
DUCTWORK	Pipes used to distribute heated or cooled air in a structure.
DURAWALL	Brand name of steel webbing placed in masonry walls to strengthen those walls.
ELEVATIONS	Drawings of the exterior of a structure.
EQUITY	The difference between what you owe on something, and what it is worth.
EXPANSION JOINT	A joint used to separate blocks or units of concrete to prevent cracking due to expansion as a result of temperature changes.
FASCIA BOARDS	The flat horizontal boards that form a band around a roof's edge.
FIRE INSURANCE	An insurance policy that protects you financially in the event of fire damage to the structure.
FIXED PRICE CONTRACT	A contractual agreement with a *general contractor* whereby, for an agreed upon price, he/she will renovate, restore, or remodel an old structure.
FLUE	A channel for the passage of hot gases and smoke.
FOOTING	A mass of concrete below the frost line supporting the foundation or piers of a house.
FRAME CONSTRUCTION	Using wood, as opposed to brick, block, concrete, or steel, for building walls, ceilings, and roofs.
FRAMING	The construction of the skeleton of a house, to include walls, floors, ceiling, and roof.
FRENCH DRAINS	Pipes placed around or under a structure to provide positive drainage of water.
FROST LINE	The depth in the earth at which the warmth of the earth prevents freezing or the formation of frost.
FURNACE	Apparatus used to heat air. It can operate on electricity, gas, or oil.
FURR OUT	Making a wall or ceiling deeper in order to provide a *chase*.
FUSES	Older safety devices that prevent electrical overloads, largely replaced by *circuit breakers*. They cannot be reused after they perform their function.
GEM's	Growth Equity Mortgage: a mortgage in which the lender shares the expected appreciation and increased *equity* of a structure. For this the lender will give a "below market" rate.
GENERAL CONTRACTOR	The person who manages the time, money, and people involved in a construction project.
GUT	To remove all the interior of a structure, except the framing.
HEAT PUMP	A heating system whereby heat is extracted from the outside air — even cold air — and used to heat a structure. Acts as air conditioning in the summer.
INSULATED GLASS	Usually refers to at least two pieces of glass with an air space in between to provide insulation.
INTERIM FINANCING	A short term loan. It is generally converted to a long term loan at a later date.
JOISTS	Horizontal framing members that comprise the floor or ceiling of a structure.
LEASE OPTION	Leasing a structure with the option to buy later at predetermined price.
LISTINGS	Pieces of real estate for sale.
LOAD BEARING CAPABILITY	The amount of weight a particular substance can withstand without breaking or bending beyond its design. Used to describe soil, steel, and wood.
LOAN CLOSING	Signing the legal documents with a lender in order to receive a loan.

LOT SUBORDINATION	A process of buying land by which the owner will take a note in lieu of payment and legally take an interest in that land secondary to a party with primary interest such as a savings and loan.
MANAGER'S CONTRACT	A contract with a general contractor by which he/she agrees to act as a manager to construct your house. Under such a contract, you remain the primary general contractor.
MOLDING	The interior trim in a house.
MORTAR	A mixture of cement, sand, and water used between bricks or concrete blocks to hold them together.
NOTE	A written acknowledgement of a debt, such as a promissory note.
PANELS	Specifically, electric panel boxes. Metal boxes that contain the *fuses* or *circuit breakers*.
PIER	A vertical structural support. Usually a masonry of metal column used to support the house, porch or deck.
PLATES	Other horizontal framing members that support walls, ceiling *joists*, of rafters. Includes *sill* plate.
PLUMB	Perfectly vertical.
POLYURETHANE	Plastic film, used in home construction to provide a moisture barrier.
PREFAB FIREPLACE	A fireplace that is made of metal instead of solid masonry. It usually has a metal flue.
PREWIRE	Wiring for various items such as lighting, telephones, intercoms, burglar alarms, and installed before drywall or paneling is applied to walls.
QUALIFIED BUYERS	Potential buyers who have already been deemed financially able to purchase a particular structure.
QUOTE	A guaranteed price in advance.
RE BARS	Steel rods placed in concrete to add strength.
RECORDING FEE	The fee charged to record legal documents in a place or permanent records, such as a county courthouse.
REINFORCING ROD	A steel rod placed in concrete to increase the strength of the concrete.
ROOF PITCH	The slope of the roof.
ROUGH-IN	The installation of wiring, plumbing, or heat ducts in the walls, floors, or ceilings before those walls, floors, or ceilings are covered with drywall, plastic, or paneling.
SAW SERVICE	Temporary electrical service used during construction.
SECOND MORTGAGE	The pledging of property to a lender as security for repayment, but using property that has already been pledged for a loan.
SEPTIC SYSTEM	A means of disposing of sewage in the ground.
SHIM	A thin wedge of wood or metal used to fill in a space.
SILL (sill plate)	A horizontal framing member, immediately adjacent to the foundation, that supports a wall or floor.
SOFFIT	The underside panel of a roof overhang or cornice.
SOFFIT VENTS	Air vents in the *soffit* to provide adequate ventilation to the framing members of the roof. Prevents rot and heat build-up.
SPECIFICATIONS	A listing of the particulars — size, quality, etc. — to be done in the renovation of the structure.
STAKING	Placing stakes in the ground prior to building to show the location of the corners of the house.
STUD	One of the uprights in the framing of a wall.
TAKE-OFF	The compilation of a list of materials used for a particular phase of construction, such as the number of bricks or the number and sizes of windows. Also called a schedule of materials.
TAMPED	Packed down. Tamping soil prevents later settling, such as underneath concrete.

TAX STAMP	A stamp affixed to a legal document to indicate that a tax has been paid.
TEST BORING	Sample of the soil on which a structure is to be built to determine what weight the soil is capable of carrying.
THERMOSTAT	A device that, based on temperature, regulates the heating and/or cooling system of a structure.
TITLE INSURANCE	An insurance policy that protects ownership of a piece of real estate. Also called "clear title."
TOPOGRAPHICAL PLAT	A drawing showing the surface features of the property.
TRANSIT	A surveying instrument used to measure horizontal angles, levelness, and vertical depth.
TRIM OUT	The stage of construction when final trim items are installed by each trade — toilets, moldings, light fixtures, etc.
UNSECURED LOAN	A loan in which no material possessions are pledged as security for repayment.
VAPOR BARRIER	A thin membrane impervious to moisture.
WATERPROOFING	Making a foundation impervious to water.
WRAPAROUND	A new loan which includes an old low interest loan, without having paid off the old loan.

Index

The numbers in boldface refer to illustrations.

Index

NATIONAL PLAN SERVICE, INC.

435 WEST FULLERTON AVE.
ELMHURST, ILLINOIS 60126
PHONE 708-833-0640

A TOTAL SERVICE TO HELP YOU PLAN YOUR NEW HOME AND HOME IMPROVEMENTS!

Over 4000 plans to choose from... for over 80 years National Plan Service has provided blueprints for residential houses to the public.

Here we are offering just a few of our best sellers and proven designs.

For a greater selection, use the convenient order form in the National Plan Service advertisement at the back of this section.

N.P.S. is way out in front in helping you... as usual!

All working drawings prepared by NATIONAL PLAN SERVICE are designed to conform to the requirements of the one and two family dwelling code (CABO) under the nationally recognized model building codes, and the U.S. Department of Housing and Urban Development's minimum property standards.

PLANS INCLUDE:

- 1/4" scale basement/foundation plan
- 1/4" scale floor plan or plans
- Full details including wall and stair sections.
- 1/4" scale exterior elevations of all four sides.
- Elevations of kitchen cabinets and bathrooms
- Locations of all electrical oulets, switches and light fixtures.
- Plumbing schematic diagram

LUMBER AND MILLWORK LIST

A complete list of all lumber and mill-work items required for the construction of the house is included with each blueprint order. Each list gives you the size and amount of materials required. It also tells you what and where the material is to be used. The list will enable you to get accurate price quotaions from several different material dealers with the knowledge that they are quoting on the same material package.

DESCRIPTION OF MATERIALS

A fill-in type description of material form is included with each plan order. This form will enable you to have a complete record of the names and accurate decription of all materials as well as model numbers of mechanical equipment to be used by your builder in the construction of your home.

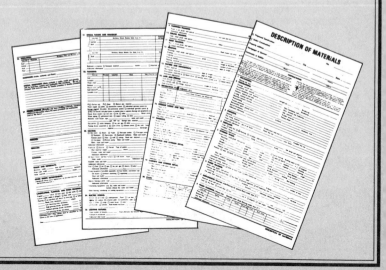

NATIONAL PLAN SERVICE

A34 A PORTFOLIO OF BEST SELLING HOUSE PLANS - all styles and sizes - Ranch, Split, 1 1/2-2 Story designs.

A35 HOME STYLE TRENDS - featuring a choice of homes of California, Contemporary and Colonial styles.

A36 BETTER LIVING HOME PLANS -a selection of brick/masonry Ranch Homes - 2,3,4,5 bedrooms.

A37 SELECTED SMALL HOMES - best selling Ranch, Split Foyer, Multi-Level, 1 1/2-2 story homes-also Narrow Lot Designs.

A39 EARLY AMERICAN COLONIAL HOMES - features ranch, 1 1/2-2 story multi-level designs.

A41 MULTI-LEVEL & HILLSIDE - exciting split foyer bi and tri levels, walk out basements.

A42 AFFORDABLE RANCH HOMES - 2,3,4 bedrooms ranch & walk out basements.

A44 ENERGY SAVING HOMES BOOK #2 - super-insulated designs full color.

A47 CONTEMPORARY HOME PLANS - Energy efficient homes- solar homes- great room concepts- contemporary designs.

A48 COUNTRY/RUSTIC HOME PLANS - a selection of rustic homes-all styles - solar homes- great room concepts.

America's Most Complete Home Planning Library

A49 THE BEST SMALL HOME PLANS - a selection of best selling small homes- all styles - 800 to 1600 Sq. Ft.

A50 VACATION HOMES - includes passive solar, year-round living, A-frames, chalets, ski-house, and contemporary designs.

A51 DUPLEX TOWNHOUSES -contains garage apartments,garden apartments, 2,3,4 and 5 unit apartments included.

A52 PRACTICAL CONTEMPORARY HOMES - a collection of proven designs, including passive solar homes, Ranches, 2-story and tri-level designs.

A55 1 1/2 -2 STORY HOMES - authentically styled Cape Cods, Garrisons, Salt Boxes, Colonials, French Provincials plus Gambrel roof styles.

A56 ENERGY SAVINGS HOME PLANS - Ranch, Split Foyer 2-Story designs, super-insulated energy cost saving plans.

A70 TUDOR HOMES & OTHER POPULAR DESIGNS - homes with Tudor influence - all styles and sizes.

A72 SUN BELT DESIGNS, OUTDOOR LIVING...INDOORS - designs featuring the open feeling of living outdoors... Vaulted ceilings, window treatments skylights and open plan designs.

A101 CUSTOM RANCH HOMES - traditional or contemporary homes for your family, areas between 1440 sq. ft. and 3108 sq. ft.

A131 OVER 100 HOME DESIGNS - includes homes for narrow lots, plan for every budget - all homes no wider than 48 feet. 88 pages.

Books of Special Interest

NPS ®

A57-GARAGE PLANS Features garages and garage apartments, studio lofts, pole buildings, machine shops and storage buildings. 20 pages. 53 plans available. **Price $3.95**

A200-BUILD YOUR OWN DECK MANUAL This book details step-by-step how to build your deck. Easy-to-follow diagrams and illustrations. Features many available Deck Plans and deck related project plans. Color. 64 pages. **Price $9.95**

SP1131-LEARN TO BE A GENERAL CONTRACTOR This book will show you how to save 25% to 30% for new and remodeled homes. How to arrange your own financing & estimating costs. Many documents and charts. 128 pages. **Price $12.95**

A100-PROJECT PLANS Includes garages, gazebos, decks, storage sheds, pole buildings, horse barns, furniture and children's projects. Over 140 projects 64 pages. Plans available. **Price $4.95.**

A270-BUILD YOUR OWN GARAGE MANUAL This book details step-by-step how to build your garage. Easy-to-follow diagrams and illustrations. Tips on garage and driveway planning. 45 garage plans available. 88 pages. **Price $12.95.**

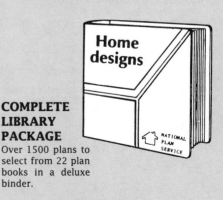